ADVOCATING
FOR
PEACE

Mennonite Reflections

Mennonite Reflections is dedicated to the publication of materials that explore the Mennonite experience. The series is published through the Institute of Anabaptist and Mennonite Studies, Conrad Grebel University College, University of Waterloo, in cooperation with Pandora Press.

The Silence Echoes: Memoirs of Trauma and Tears
    Edited and translated by Sarah Dyck, 1997

Lifting the Veil: Mennonite Life in Russia Before the Revolution
    Jacob H. Janzen. Edited with an introduction by Leonard Friesen. Translated by Walter Klaassen, 1998

A *Life Displaced: A Mennonite Woman's Flight from War-Torn Poland*
    Edna Schroeder Thiessen, 2000

Mennonite Alternative Service in Russia: The Story of Abram Dück and His Colleagues 1911-1917
    John Dick and Lawrence Klippenstein, 2002

The Plain People: A Glimpse at Life among the Old Order Mennonites of Ontario
    John F. Peters, 2003

From Kleefeld with Love
    John A. Harder, 2003

Old Order Mennonites of Ontario: Gelassenheit, Discipleship, Brotherhood
    Donald Martin, 2003

Pioneers in Ministry: Women Pastors in Ontario Mennonite Churches
    Mary A. Schiedel, 2003

A Family Torn Apart
    Justina A. Neufeld, 2003

Between Worlds: Reflections of a Soviet-born Canadian Mennonite
    Harry Loewen, 2006

Strange and Wonderful Paths: The Memoirs of Ralph Lebold
    Ralph Lebold, 2006

Among the Ashes: In the Stalinkova Kolkhoz
    Edited, translated and commentary by Peter J. Rahn, 2011

Howard Raid: Man of Faith and Vision
    Elizabeth Raid, 2011

The Orie O. Miller Diary: 1920-21
    Orie O. Miller, 2018

Advocating for Peace: Stories from the Ottawa Office of Mennonite Central Committe, 1975–2008
    William Janzen, 2019

ADVOCATING FOR PEACE

Stories from the Ottawa Office
of Mennonite Central Committee
1975 – 2008

William Janzen

Library and Archives Canada Cataloguing in Publication

Title: Advocating for peace : stories from the Ottawa office of Mennonite Central Committee,
   1975-2008 / William Janzen.
Names: Janzen, William, 1943- author.
Identifiers: Canadiana 20190226129 | ISBN 9781926599663 (softcover)
Subjects: LCSH: Janzen, William, 1943-—Anecdotes. | LCSH: Mennonite Central Committee Canada—
   Anecdotes. | LCSH: Mennonite Central Committee Canada—Employees—Anecdotes. | LCSH: Mennonite
   Central Committee Canada—History. | LCSH: Mennonites—Ontario—Ottawa—Anecdotes. | LCGFT:
   Anecdotes.
Classification: LCC BX8118.5 .J36 2019 | DDC 289.7/71—dc23

Book design by Christian Snyder

ADVOCATING FOR PEACE.
ISBN 978-1-926599-66-3
Copyright © 2019 Pandora Press
   Published by Pandora Press
   47 Water Street North
   Kitchener, Ontario N2H 5A6
All rights reserved.

www.pandorapress.com
All Pandora Press publications are printed in Canada on FSC certified paper.

28 27 26 25 24 23 22 21 20 19   1 2 3 4 5 6 7 8 9 10

To Marlene Toews Janzen, a teacher at a Mennonite high school in Winnipeg who was appointed to the MCCC board in 1980 and who, two years later, agreed to marry me. For her steady support in the work and her encouragement in our life together, I will always be grateful.

Contents

♦

Foreword	9
Introduction	13
Letters to New Prime Ministers	19
Capital Punishment	25
Refugees	28
Foreign Policy, Development, and Peace	39
Vietnam and Cambodia	49
Palestine and Israel	63
Iraq	75
North Korea	88
The USSR	91
Other International Work	98
Canadian Constitutional Reform	103
War Criminals	107
Abortion	114
Conscientious Objection	118
Other Social Issues	123
Amish Milk Cans	128
Organizational Maintenance	132
Mennonites from Mexico	138
Conclusion	166

Foreword

◆

In 1975, Mennonite Central Committee Canada established the Ottawa Office to monitor and interpret government policy for its Mennonite and Brethren in Christ constituency, and to undertake advocacy to government on behalf of its national and international programs. William Janzen was the first director of MCC's Ottawa Office, a position he held for thirty-three years. In this volume, he shares a rich collection of stories from those years of "advocating for peace."

The emergence of the Ottawa Office marked a significant shift in MCC's mission of addressing human need. Prior to the 1970s, MCC had worked primarily through the distribution of material aid and through the hands-on engagement of service workers in health, agriculture, education and other forms of community development. The Ottawa Office symbolized MCC's recognition that relieving human suffering also involved addressing government policy.[*]

As Janzen notes, if Mennonites were ready to go to Ottawa to advocate for themselves—which they had done in numerous contexts—they should do it for others as well. Also important was the growing sense that advocacy to government was an important way of challenging structural and systemic injustice.

The fifty stories included in this volume reflect the vast range

---

[*] A similar office had been established in Washington, DC in 1968.

of issues upon which Janzen and his colleagues worked. These issues included conscientious objection, the arms trade and nuclear weapons; Canada's foreign policy in Vietnam and Cambodia, Palestine and Israel, North Korea and Iraq; international aid and support for refugees; constitutional reform; capital punishment; war criminals; and Amish milk cans—to name only a few.

The stories also portray the many different ways Janzen engaged in advocacy—whether writing extensive letters to prime ministers; crafting detailed submissions to parliamentary committees; building relationships with key Members of Parliament and civil servants; or hosting meetings and consultations. They reveal the unique advocacy style which Janzen and other staff came to embody: a posture of patience and humility; a practice of detailed research, consultation and analysis; and a principled commitment to non-partisanship.

Janzen is quick to admit the work of the Ottawa Office did not always lead to the kind of policy change for which MCC hoped. Nevertheless, given the size of the office during much of Janzen's time—one director, an assistant and an occasional intern—its impact has been considerable, as these stories show. One instance with immediate results relates to the office's involvement in negotiating Canada's first master agreement for the private sponsorship of refugees. The structure resulting from this agreement enabled countless people to become active in helping to resettle refugees.

Advocating for Peace reflects a particular era—an era in which church-based agencies like MCC were generally respected in government and therefore gained relatively easy access to Members of Parliament and senior government officials. It also reflects a time in which MCC member churches more readily looked to the Ottawa Office to speak on their behalf—including their concerns about moral issues such as abortion, divorce, and even smoking. As Janzen notes in his conclusions, that era has passed, though advocacy is needed more than ever.

The Christian calling to love and care for the neighbour demands many varieties of response. Advocacy is one of them. Readers of

Advocating for Peace will find here a rich history of the Christian advocacy undertaken by MCC's Ottawa Office during its first three decades. Hopefully, they will be inspired to embrace new forms of advocacy in the future.

Esther Epp-Tiessen
August, 2019

Introduction

◆

In 2008, when I retired as the director of the Ottawa Office of Mennonite Central Committee Canada (MCCC), my supervisors, Don Peters and Lois Coleman Neufeld, encouraged me to write up stories about the work I'd done. At first I hesitated; some parts of the work seemed too complex; other parts too mundane; and altogether it was so diverse. How could one present it in the form of stories? But when I reviewed the reports that I had written for the MCCC Board over the years I began to feel that perhaps something could be pulled together. So I made an outline and started writing. Then one aspect of the citizenship work with the Mennonites from Mexico became much, much larger than I expected, as is described near the end of this collection. Eventually, however, I was able to return to this project.

This collection of stories may look like a personal memoir, but I believe it is more. The work was not mine personally; it was that of MCCC and its supporting churches which, in those years, numbered approximately 600. And since it involved issues of government, it was a particular kind of work. Not that appealing to governments was new to Mennonites. They had done it for centuries. But most often they had done it for themselves, asking for land where they could settle and build their communities, for exemption from military service, and sometimes for special schooling arrangements. By the 1970s, however, MCCC felt that it should also appeal to governments for the sake of other people. Mennonites had a considerable history of working to alleviate the needs of others in hands-on practical ways, but to appeal to government for the sake of other people was relatively new. The Ottawa Office was a primary mechanism to advance this purpose. These stories capture some of what that involved.

This new orientation in MCCC was in keeping with other changes. Canadian Mennonite people were moving to cities, seeking more education, and entering more professions. As well, they were taking on more governing responsibilities by, for example, getting elected at municipal, provincial and federal levels and serving as civil servants, even as judges. The historic virtue of "being separate" was receding and the work of helping to provide good governance in the larger society was more widely accepted. There were other new winds. The role of American church leaders in the US civil rights movement and in the opposition to the US war in Vietnam inspired many. In Canada, Protestant churches were looking anew at the causes of poverty and injustice both at home and abroad. And the Catholic world, helped by the Second Vatican Council of the mid-1960s, was changing too. This ferment led to the formation of a number of Canadian ecumenical coalitions to do research and advocacy on issues of justice and peace.

MCCC had already taken steps in this new direction in the late 1960s and early 1970s. It had participated in some ecumenical initiatives and sponsored certain activities in Ottawa on its own, including research projects on immigration and military issues. However, the question of establishing an Office in Ottawa was viewed with caution. Alongside hopes that such an Office would significantly advance work on peace and justice issues, there were fears that it would address political issues in ways that would cause division among the churches which, only in 1963, had joined in forming MCCC. Despite these misgivings, in 1974 the MCCC board decided to set up an Ottawa Office for a three-year trial period. I started work in 1975, not altogether confident about how to deal with the different concerns at a practical level.

In preparation I read as widely as I could, about Mennonite theological perspectives, about the work of other churches including that of the Social Gospel movement early in the 20th century, and about a range of current political issues. Before long I also learned that there were significant organizational complexities in MCCC. In these years MCCC was setting up other offices too, including an Aboriginal Concerns office, a Victim-Offender Ministries office, and an Overseas Services office, each with a mandate that included advocacy on the governmental aspects of their issues. In addition, MCCC was in several coalitions such as Project Ploughshares which worked on issues of militarism. This meant that quite a lot of MCCC's governmental work was being done by these offices and coalitions. What role then could the Ottawa Office play? Would I be able to help those other offices with the governmental aspects of their work? Were there issues not covered by those other offices that MCCC would want me to work on? One conclusion I drew is that I would have to be flexible and quick to adapt.

The ambiguities about my role continued, but as one year led to the next and the next, I always felt that what I was able to do was genuinely worthwhile and that, despite some frustrations, I was fortunate for the opportunity to be in this work. But it remained very diverse. That is evident in this collection of stories. Some stories reflect a short term involvement. Others are about work that went on for years. The issues include matters of war and peace, international relief and development, refugee needs, Canadian domestic issues, and various aspects of MCC's service programs at home and abroad. At times MCC also wanted to address issues because of the concern about them in its supporting churches, or the implications they had for MCC as an organization, or the historic desire to help fellow Mennonites in difficult situations.

Even though these stories cover a range of activities, this collection is not a full history of the Ottawa Office. It does not cover my work of representing MCC on the boards and committees of various coalitions nor with that of writing for Mennonite publications or speaking in churches. It deals primarily with advocacy activities where I had a direct role and only with those that lend themselves to stories. In total there are about fifty stories. They are organized thematically, not chronologically. Each issue discussed in these stories has an historical and political context. Also, in many instances MCC was working on issues with its on-the-ground service programs. I have tried, for each issue, to describe enough of the historical context and enough of MCC's broader involvement, to make our Ottawa work understandable.

Writing up these stories has reminded me of my indebtedness to countless people. Unfortunately, I can mention only a few. First are my assistants. For most of my years I had only one, but the three people who served in this role the longest are Freda Enns, Joanne Epp, and Monica Scheifele. Second are my supervisors, J. M. Klassen, Daniel Zehr, Marvin Frey, Dave Dyck, and the two mentioned at the outset. Third are several people on the MCCC board who, in my early years, provided special support. These include Frank Epp, Siegfried Bartel, and Leonard Siemens. Also to be thanked are the churches whose steady support made this work possible.

In many instances the issues we worked on have not gone away. Some, such as global hunger, have eased, but refugee numbers are way up and war, now often within countries rather than between them, continues, while climate change is adding major new dimensions. These developments make it all the more important that people of goodwill respond as fully as possible. Perhaps these stories can encourage people to do that through whatever avenues may be open to them, including that of supporting modest organizations like Mennonite Central Committee.

Some people may wonder about the name: is it MCCC or MCC? In a strict sense I was employed by the MCCC organization that is,

Introduction 17

Mennonite Central Committee Canada. But it is very common to refer to it as MCC since it is an integral part of the family of MCC organizations, the first of which was started in 1920 as a joint effort by churches in the US and Canada. Both the specific and the general uses of the term are evident in these stories.

The publication of this book was helped by a modest grant from MCCC while Christian Snyder of Pandora Press did the detailed work of seeing it through. I am greatful to both.

William Janzen
Ottawa, Ontario
February 2019

1

LETTERS TO NEW PRIME MINISTERS

◆

*I*n Europe, from the 16th century to the 19th, when new rulers came to power in countries where the Mennonites lived, they would often seek meetings with them. The Mennonites wanted the new rulers to know who they were, to express gratitude for being allowed to live there, to explain their loyalty, and to seek assurances that they would not have to serve in the military.

To an extent Mennonites continued the practice of meeting with leaders when they moved to Canada. Indeed, in the 1820s when Christian Nafziger, an Amish leader from Bavaria, sought new settlement opportunities in Upper Canada, he stopped in London, England and reportedly met with King George IV, who then gave him the desired assurances of full religious freedom. In the two world wars of the twentieth century, delegations from different Mennonite groups came to Ottawa to plead for military exemption, and, in the case of World War II, to arrange for a national alternative service program. In the decades that followed, Mennonite leaders met with a series of new Prime Ministers, including Louis St-Laurent in 1951, John Diefenbaker in 1959, Lester Pearson in 1965, and Pierre Trudeau in 1970.

All of these developments were before my time in the Ottawa

Office, but the 1970 meeting with Mr. Trudeau is noteworthy. MCCC had prepared a substantial letter for presentation to him. It expressed gratitude that over the years Canadian governments had opened doors for Mennonite immigrants and refugees despite some pressures not to do so, and that generally they had provided for conscientious objection to military service and allowed alternative service. The letter then asked for assistance with getting Mennonite relatives from the Soviet Union to Canada, and for an exemption for Amish and Old Order Mennonites from the newly enacted Canada Pension Plan, both of which were concerns at that time. Further, indicating a broader agenda, the letter indicated support for the admission of American draft-age immigrants and others fleeing war and persecution, for the establishment of official ties with the People's Republic of China while maintaining similar ties with Taiwan, for increased international development work, for reduced military spending, and for endowing university chairs in "peace studies". Finally, the letter called on Canada to "lead the world in backing away from its military madness."

When Mennonite leaders first asked for a meeting with Mr. Trudeau, they were refused. Mr. Trudeau may have felt that then he'd have to meet with all kinds of small groups. But when his refusals became public and he happened to be travelling through Winnipeg for other reasons, a meeting was quickly arranged. It turned out to be remarkably positive. According to the report, Mr. Trudeau said:

> I don't think I've ever received a more beautiful brief. Most of the ideas in here, or feelings, are ones which are very close to my own heart. I am very sensitive to a brief which begins by offering me only good wishes, [and] prayers, and I thank you very much.

In 1979, when Joe Clark became Prime Minister, the MCCC Ottawa Office was in place. I was then asked to prepare a substantial letter and to ask for a meeting. Then an unexpected election intervened and the requested meeting did not take place. That election, in early 1980, brought Pierre Trudeau back to power. We then modified the letter and sent it to him though we did not press for another meeting.

In 1984 when Brian Mulroney came to power, I again prepared a substantial letter in consultation with colleagues and leaders in our churches. The letter had a paragraph on each of the following issues: military exemption, immigration and refugee matters, relations with the "eastern bloc", foreign policy generally, defence matters, overseas aid, Canada's indigenous people, criminal justice matters, people with disabilities, and abortion.

Interestingly, Mr. Mulroney's office passed the letter on to Mr. Clark, now External Affairs minister, who then responded warmly, particularly on those matters relating to foreign affairs, stating in part:

> First, however, I would like to express my admiration for the very notable contributions that the Mennonite community has made to Canada over the years. As a Western Canadian I am very much aware of these, especially the Community's consistent advocacy of social justice and peace.... I can assure you that arms control and disarmament constitute a major Government priority, and my Department will be looking for every opportunity to exert a positive influence on the climate and substance of negotiations. We want to help build an international environment in which acceptable means of conflict resolution increasingly replace military solutions.

In addition to the letter's primary audience, we sent copies to several dozen Members of Parliament whose constituencies included a significant number of Mennonites. Many of these MPs responded with more than an acknowledgement. David Orlikow from Winnipeg wrote:

> I have gone through the points you raise and the position you take on very important issues. I find that I am in agreement with all the views which you have expressed

and can assure you that whenever possible I will keep the views you have expressed in mind....

Svend Robinson from British Columbia wrote:

... Thank you very much for the copy of your thoughtful letter ... I share many of the concerns your committee has outlined, and the recommendations designed to build a more just and humane community, at both a national and international level. In particular, your submission makes eloquent reference to the urgent need for better understanding between 'east and west', for greater emphasis on Canada's tradition of honourable mediation in the international arena, and for increased aid ... for the less fortunate nations of the world.

Ernie Epp from Thunder Bay said:

I did find the letter very interesting and was pleased to see the various points on which we are in sympathy. My Mennonite heritage is still a motive element in my public life.

Barry Turner from Ottawa-Carleton wrote this:

Overall you and your colleagues are to be congratulated for the tone of the letter. It is thoughtful and representative, yet not hard or fanatical.

Ray Hnatyshyn from Saskatoon wrote:

I very much appreciate the comments and opinions of the Committee on the many matters raised in the letter ...

Kim Campbell became Prime Minister in 1993 but she did not serve long, so we did not get a letter in to her. That fall, when Jean Chrétien became Prime Minister, I was on a leave but MCCC sent in a substantial brief dealing with peace, security, international development, refugees, indigenous people, violence against women, and unemployment. This letter also asked for a provision to allow people to redirect a percentage of their income tax, equal to the percentage of the federal budget used for defence, so that that money would then be used for a different purpose. The brief also asked for a meeting with Mr. Chrétien but none took place.

After Paul Martin came to power, in 2003, we again sent a letter but not one with a full list of issues. Instead, we introduced the Mennonite people of Canada, made some references to our theology, our history, the global Mennonite community, and the work of MCC. Then we elaborated on two global issues: poverty and security, pleading for strong and imaginative action on both. Interestingly, this letter was signed not only by the chair of MCCC but also by the moderators of the seven Mennonite denominations that were members of MCCC at that time.

The 2006 letter to Stephen Harper was only one page. We introduced the Mennonites and the work of MCC and explained the faith underlying the work in the following way:

> a faith that God is at work seeking to restore the world, including creation itself, for the well-being of all people, including those who are marginalized and in situations of enmity.... With this in mind, we will, from time to time, seek to share perspectives and concerns that arise from our work with representatives of your government, in the hope of contributing to policies that address the profound challenges of our world.

In my view, these communications reflect a notable evolution in the context. Centuries ago kings and czars often dealt with things personally. Their bureaucracies were much smaller and there were fewer laws and regulations. A great deal depended on the personal word of the rulers. In such contexts it was important that rulers have some understanding of the Mennonites and their concerns. In our time rulers are more circumscribed; they have to work within a more elaborate context of laws, regulations, administrative bodies, and officials. They will not respond single-handedly to a broad range of issues. This also means that communications and appeals have to be addressed to many different points in government.

Nevertheless, I believe our introductory letters to new Prime Ministers had positive effects, perhaps less in the immediate purpose of challenging Prime Ministers than in building relations with Members of Parliament and civil servants to whom we sent copies. Also, by preparing such letters in broad consultation with Mennonite leaders, they became a means of expressing how the Canadian Mennonite people saw themselves. They helped to articulate, and thereby to build, a self-understanding and a common approach to the world.

2

CAPITAL PUNISHMENT

◆

The issue of capital punishment was debated twice during my years with MCC's Ottawa Office—in 1976 and in 1987. But there had been no executions in Canada since 1962. Even before that, the federal cabinet had often commuted death sentences to life imprisonment. In 1963, the government of Lester Pearson made such commutations a matter of executive policy. In 1967, at Pearson's initiative, Parliament passed a law placing a five-year moratorium on all executions, except for the killing of police officers and prison guards. In 1972, that moratorium was renewed for another five years. In 1976, before that moratorium expired, Prime Minister Pierre Trudeau decided that either capital punishment would be formally abolished or it would be enforced. His government then introduced a bill to abolish it.

How would MCC respond? Significantly, in 1973 the board of MCCC had formally adopted a statement against capital punishment. This made it easier for us to work on this issue, although people in the churches were not of one mind on it. We then sent a letter and the 1973 MCCC statement to a number of Members of Parliament. One Mennonite MP, Bill Andres from Niagara-on-the-Lake, asked us for copies of a 1965 pamphlet by the General Conference Mennonite Church. He then sent one to each of his fellow MPs. We also helped two Ontario Mennonite bodies—the Western Ontario

Mennonite Conference and the United Mennonite Conference of Ontario, both of which were later absorbed into Mennonite Church Eastern Canada—who wanted to equip their people to write letters to their Members of Parliament opposing capital punishment. Also, I wrote a lengthy article for the Mennonite press weighing the different arguments. Many Canadians became engaged on this issue. They wrote to their MPs. When the Parliamentary vote was held on July 14, 1976, the abolition side carried, but only by six votes.

The second debate took place in 1987. The Progressive Conservative party, which had come to power in 1984, had committed itself to allowing a free vote on the issue. However, the Prime Minister, Brian Mulroney, an abolitionist himself, was in no hurry. It was not until 1987 that he introduced a motion in the House of Commons. At first it appeared that a substantial majority of MPs would vote to reinstate capital punishment, but that did not happen. Many churches, organizations, and individuals wrote to their MPs. The lobbying was intense. We prepared a two-page letter for the signature of MCCC chair Ray Brubacher, and sent it to all MPs. Our letter referred to the 1973 MCC statement, to MCC's growing work with offenders and victims, to the question of whether capital punishment was a deterrent, and to other arguments. MCCC also supported the ecumenical coalition, the Church Council on Justice and Corrections, in its lobbying work.

While working on this issue, I remembered that on my very first visit to Ottawa in 1966, I had listened to the debate on Pearson's bill for the five-year moratorium; more specifically, I was in the House of Commons Gallery when the Rt. Hon. John Diefenbaker, then leader of the Progressive Conservative party, gave a major speech against capital punishment, meaning that he supported Pearson's moratorium. I now dug out that speech, printed it in pamphlet form using the title "John Diefenbaker Against Capital Punishment," and sent it to many Members of Parliament, including many who favoured capital punishment but who generally saw Diefenbaker as a hero. When the vote was held on June 30, 1987, the abolitionist side again carried the day, this time by 21 votes.

Unlike many issues where I appealed to civil servants and Ministers, the capital punishment issue lay entirely with elected Members of Parliament. All appeals had to be directed to them. One MP, upon welcoming me into his office, said, "Bill, if you're coming to tell me that the Mennonites of Canada are against capital punishment, I'll show you a stack of letters with a different message." His comments were a helpful reminder not to overstate my role. Another MP said: "I don't like it that you abolitionists talk as if you are following your consciences and imply that others of us are not. I am not happy about executing people but I believe society should reserve for itself the right to impose the ultimate penalty." Another MP, an abolitionist, noted, "80% of my constituents have always disagreed with me on this issue but they keep voting for me." He explained "on this issue public opinion is a mile wide but only an inch deep." Certainly, the end result was a reminder that the work of letter writing, talking with MPs, and doing the research and analysis can make a difference. A good number of MPs changed their mind.

3

REFUGEES

◆

Refugee resettlement work has deep roots among Mennonite people in Canada. In the 1920s the Canadian Mennonite Board of Colonization, the first national inter-Mennonite organization, resettled some 21,000 Mennonite refugees from the Soviet Union. Another 7,800 were admitted to Canada after World War II.

Canadian Mennonites were not involved in a major way with helping to resettle the refugees who came from Hungary in 1956, or those from Czechoslovakia in 1968, or the Asians from Uganda in 1972. Other groups seemed to be dealing with these needs. However, late in the 1970s, Mennonites responded substantially to the refugee crisis in Southeast Asia. In the following decade, they opened their doors to people from Central America, many of whom had fled to the US but were not free to stay there. Canadian Mennonites have continued to assist in the resettlement of people from Africa, the Middle East, and other places.

The role of MCCC, and that of the provincial MCC organizations, has been one of facilitating this work. The main energy for it has come from Mennonite churches across the country. They have set up committees, provided the funds, and done the daily work of helping newcomers. In several cities, they have set up sizable refugee centres with a range of programs. In the total context, the role of MCC's Ottawa Office was quite minor but at some points it was important.

Negotiating the Master Agreement in 1979

By 1978, there was widespread concern in Canadian Mennonite churches about the "boat people" from Vietnam. People from Vietnam, some of them ethnic Chinese, were fleeing in small boats in the hope of gaining temporary asylum in a nearby country and then permanent resettlement elsewhere. Mennonites knew about Vietnam. MCC had had programs there since 1954, becoming a leading Protestant relief agency by the mid-1960s when the US military involvement was so massive. Most of MCC's work was in South Vietnam but it also sent some medical supplies to the communist north and it continued to send relief shipments after North Vietnam took over South Vietnam in 1975. But the plight of these people, seen on the daily news across Canada, added a whole new dimension. They were risking everything. It is believed that tens of thousands died at sea. What gave the matter urgency was that neighbouring countries like Thailand, Malaysia, and Indonesia, afraid of being flooded with these migrants, were starting to say that they would stop providing temporary refuge for them if the international community did not promise to accept them for permanent resettlement.

This was the context for the annual meeting of MCCC held in Calgary on January 19 and 20, 1979. There was a strong request that I, upon my return to Ottawa, work out an arrangement with the Immigration department so that Mennonite congregations across Canada could start bringing over these refugees. Canada's new immigration law, which had come into force on April 1, 1978, had a small provision for the private sponsorship of refugees. Any five individuals could sponsor a refugee if they assumed full responsibility, including legal liability, for one year. Some groups took up the challenge, but many hesitated because of the liability question and what it might mean if things did not work out.

When I then returned to Ottawa, I called Cal Best who, I believe, was an Assistant Deputy Minister at the time. I had recently had dealings with him on other matters. He was most receptive, confident that a mutually satisfactory arrangement could be worked out. His openness may have been helped by the emerging public pressure, including that from MPs like Jake Epp and Doug Roche. Cal Best and I agreed to hold a substantial meeting on February 2, 1979. John Wieler and Art Driedger from MCC's Overseas Services department in Winnipeg joined us for this meeting, as did several colleagues from Ottawa. The Immigration officials talked about the new law's provisions for private sponsorship and for making a "designated class." The latter, they explained, gave them more flexibility than the strict definition of the UN Convention for Refugees. We then talked about an agreement in broad terms, after which Gordon Barnett from the government's side, and I from MCC's side, were to flesh it out and write it up.

Gordon and I met a number of times over the next few weeks, always checking with our respective colleagues. The negotiations progressed well. On March 5, 1979, our Executive Director, J. M. Klassen, and the Minister, the Hon. Bud Cullen, signed the agreement in MCC's Winnipeg offices. It was called a Master Agreement (MA) because of its umbrella function. The essence was simple. MCCC as a national organization would now accept full liability for any church or group of people whom it authorized to sponsor refugees. The individual churches would carry all the regular resettlement costs but they would not be left liable if exceptional problems developed. This arrangement also assured officials that any groups authorized by MCCC would be able to carry through. They would not have to screen them. Further, the MA created a "joint assistance" track for special needs cases. And it outlined the flow of communications, from MCCC to a church group in Canada, to a local Immigration office, to Immigration headquarters in Ottawa, to the Embassies in Southeast Asia, indicating what was to happen at each stage. Email had not yet been invented.

Soon after MCCC signed the MA, over half the 600 Mennonite

and Brethren in Christ congregations in Canada submitted applications to sponsor refugees. And in the next weeks and months, some two dozen other national church bodies and dioceses signed virtually identical agreements with the Immigration department. In June 1979, Operation Lifeline was started in Toronto by Professor Howard Adelman and in July, Ottawa's mayor, Marion Dewar, launched Project 4000. According to the 2017 book, *Running on Empty: Canada and the Indochinese Refugee Crisis, 1975 – 1980*, the "sponsorship commitments" of private groups "exceeded the most optimistic expectations" (p. 155). This also led the government to vastly increase the number that it would sponsor, despite an ambivalence in public opinion. As recently as June 1979, Canada was planning to take in a total of only 12,000 (8,000 government sponsored and 4,000 privately) but in late July, Flora MacDonald, Minister of External Affairs, supported by Prime Minister Joe Clark, raised the total number to 50,000. As a result, from 1975 to the end of 1980 Canada brought in 70,000, approximately one-half of whom were privately sponsored (p. 104-121). (According to Mike Molloy, a senior Immigration official, MacDonald's commitment to 50,000 was probably influenced by John Wieler's use of that number when he was interviewed in the July 16, 1979 issue of *Maclean's* magazine.) Mennonite church groups sponsored approximately 5,000.

Years later, Gordon Barnett told me of an interesting development on his side. He had been instructed to negotiate so that MCC would be left carrying as many responsibilities as possible and the government as few as possible. After we started meeting, however, he took a different approach. In *Running on Empty*, Gordon is quoted as saying: "Bill negotiated in such good faith it was embarrassing to play the cards I had been given.... Negotiating with MCC demonstrated only their complete commitment to help, against our reluctance to give anything up and our meanness. I thought we should adopt a different, more cooperative approach.... It may well be that had the first agreement not been negotiated with a group as openly altruistic and sincerely helpful as MCC, the

National Sponsorship Agreements would have been less cooperative" (p.76). The book goes on to say, "the private sponsorship program ... has been frequently examined by other governments seeking to strengthen their resettlement programs, but it has not been easy to transplant it elsewhere, less because of its design than because of the value system that underpins it" (p. 81).

After the MA was signed, my role was greatly reduced, though I helped with some detailed issues. Most of the work on our side was now done by staff in Winnipeg and the provincial MCCs, and particularly by people in the churches. On the field, MCC workers and Embassy officials cooperated so well that for a while MCC had a desk inside the Canadian Embassy in Bangkok. Regarding the larger Canadian churches, at first some of them were a bit critical, saying that by taking on this work as a church we had let the government "off the hook." Soon, however, that view faded as the volume of private sponsorship work prompted the government to increase its own.

Though the Master Agreement model for the private sponsorship of refugees worked well, soon the first arrivals began to ask the churches who had sponsored them to now also sponsor their relatives and family members. Many churches were willing to help, but officials were not keen on this. They felt that if private groups could "name" the people they wanted to sponsor, then their capacity to respond simply on a "needs" basis would be restricted. Other factors also changed, and the initial enthusiasm waned. Nevertheless, private sponsorship by churches has remained important. In 2016 it had a large role in bringing over Syrian refugees, and that role appears to be continuing.

In 1986 the UN awarded the Nansen Medal to The People of Canada for their very substantial response to the Vietnamese refugee crisis. One Canadian official thought the award should have gone to MCC. Raphael Girard recently told me that he had recommended to the UNHCR that they give the medal MCC in recognition of its refugee work both in Canada and in various places overseas. However flattering that might have been, by awarding the medal to the people of Canada, the UNHCR wisely extended its affirmation and encouragement more broadly. Would that such acknowledgement of refugee resettlement work were accompanied by an awareness of the people who did not get out and, more generally, of the factors that cause so many people to become refugees in the first place. I am grateful that MCC has been active not only with refugees but also with people in Vietnam.

Keeping "Inland Determination" Open, 1987

For the "boat people" from Southeast Asia, the decisions about which refugees to admit were made on the field, based on interviews and medical examinations done there. But there was another avenue for desperate people to seek legal status in Canada. They could come to a Canadian point of entry, such as an airport, and claim to be refugees as defined by the UN Convention for Refugees. Since Canada had signed that Convention in 1967 and especially after the 1985 Supreme Court ruling in the Singh case, Canada had a legal obligation to grant hearings to such claimants. This was referred to as "inland determination." The people were called "asylum seekers" or "inland refugee claimants."

Until late into the 1970s, Canada had very few inland refugee claimants, largely because Canada was so remote that it was difficult for people to get here. But the Immigration Act of 1978 created a Refugee Status Advisory Committee (RSAC) to deal with the claimants who did come. At first the RSAC dealt with only a small number of cases per year. However, in 1981 there were 1600 such claims and in 1986 there were 18,000. Since the RSAC system was not capable of dealing with such numbers, a huge backlog developed. People in it were holding jobs and starting families, hoping that eventually they would be given the right to live here permanently. Critics said that for some the inland claimant route had become an easy immigration avenue.

What to do? Most of those already here would eventually be allowed to stay, but the government was determined to stop the flow, so in 1987 it introduced Bill C – 55. This Bill would create the

Immigration and Refugee Board (IRB) for the purpose of hearing inland claimants, but it also proposed mechanisms so that not all claimants would get a full hearing on the substance of their claim. Among other things, claimants could be denied a full hearing if they originated from a country deemed to have a generally good human rights record, and therefore not likely to produce genuine refugees, and those who came via a safe third country, that is, a country where it was believed they could have obtained a hearing. The government also introduced Bill C – 84, which gave the minister the authority to interdict ships suspected of carrying claimants to Canada.

These bills led to heated public discussion in the summer of 1987. Quite a few of the asylum seekers who came in those years were from Central America, where civil wars were raging; would Canada close its door on them? A number of groups appeared before the Parliamentary Committee studying these bills; some groups argued fervently about what principles of justice and international laws should be followed. To prepare for our appearance, scheduled for the evening of September 2, I worked closely with Stuart Clark, MCCC's Winnipeg-based Refugee Coordinator. We then invited David Janzen, coordinator of the "Overground Railroad" in the US, and Carmen Albrecht, who had served with MCC in Guatemala for three years and now worked with a refugee program in Kitchener, Ontario.

In our presentation we reviewed MCCC's refugee work in general and then focused on our current involvement with people from Central America who had fled to the US. Since their chances of being given refugee status in the US were very slim, our partners in the US had helped many to apply for refugee status at Canadian Consulates in the US, particularly the one in Dallas, Texas. We were able to report that the officials there had shown themselves to be quite sympathetic. Then we described other cases where the people, for various reasons, could not apply through the Consulates; they needed to get to a Canadian entry point and make an inland claim. We pointed out how aspects of the proposed legislation could prevent such people from getting a hearing.

Fortunately, we had the Committee to ourselves that evening. The news media were preoccupied with the appearance of former Prime Minister Pierre Trudeau elsewhere on the Hill. This may have helped to depoliticize our session. And with David Janzen and Carmen Albrecht we were able to talk about the situation of actual people, not just about principles and laws. We were also able to show that we, like the government, preferred to process applications through Consulates and Embassies abroad, but that for some people making an inland claim was the only option and that some aspects of the proposed legislation could close doors for such people.

Soon after our appearance before the Parliamentary Committee, two letters of appreciation came to our office. One was from a government MP who, by reputation, was the most fervent defender of the legislation and the strongest critic of groups who pressed for changes. The other was from Opposition MP Dan Heap, who said that after our presentation, that government MP had adopted a much more constructive tone. Perhaps our moderate approach, emphasizing "hands-on" work with actual cases, and expressing appreciation for officials at the Consulates, was effective. We did further work in talking with MPs individually. In the end, the government changed a number of the points about which we and other groups had raised the strongest concern.

Further Work on "Inland Determination," 1992

In June 1992, the government proposed a new immigration law, Bill C – 86. It dealt with immigration generally. Among other things, it provided for speedier processing of family class cases, allowed for special programs, promised more flexibility with regard to medical criteria, and enabled people who had been approved as refugees to bring their dependents over more quickly.

These points were positive, but with regard to inland refugee claimants this bill sought again to restrict access to the IRB. In part this was understandable—the number of such claimants had risen to over 30,000 annually. For the IRB to hear so many cases was costly. With this bill the government would give Senior Immigration Officers the authority to bar people who had come via a "prescribed" country, a new term that included the meaning of "safe third country," from getting to the IRB. The bill also required that in order to get a hearing, claimants had to have come with valid passports or other travel documents. People with a criminal record could also be barred.

I then asked for an opportunity to appear before the Senate committee studying the bill. To prepare, I contacted people who were directly involved with refugees, namely Rudy Baergen, senior minister at First Mennonite Church in Kitchener; Betty Puricelli from the New Life Centre in Toronto; and John Doherty from the Mennonite House of Friendship in Montreal. They joined me before the Senate committee on September 4, 1992. The title of our 16-page brief was "Love the Sojourner ... For You Were Sojourners," taken from the Bible, Deuteronomy 10:19.

These three individuals provided ten stories of refugees with whom they had been involved. On that basis, we then spoke to several elements in the bill. Regarding the "safe third country" concept, if this were implemented, we said, then many refugees would be at the mercy of the seriously inadequate system in the US. Regarding the requirement that refugees come with proper documentation, we said that for many an attempt to get passports from their own governments would be to risk their lives. Regarding the exclusion of anyone believed to have been convicted of a crime, we asked if Canadian authorities would rely on information about any convictions on the person's home government from which the person was fleeing. We also asked for a procedure to appeal IRB rulings. We acknowledged that the number of claimants had risen substantially, but noted that it was still well below that of many other refugee-receiving countries.

I recall that the Senate committee listened attentively and asked good questions. My 1992 annual report to the MCCC board states: "The Senate Committee's report, released in mid-September, reflected many of the concerns that we and other groups raised." It can also be noted that while we spoke against the idea of a safe third country agreement with the US, in 2004 the federal government did make such an agreement, though it was not as rigid as originally envisioned.

Appeals on Behalf of Individuals
A number of times, when people had managed to get to Canada but had been refused by the IRB, I was asked to submit their cases to the Minister who had the power to approve them on "humanitarian and compassionate" (H & C) grounds. One such case in 2006 involved a young Muslim man from Turkey. He was seeking Permanent Resident status in Canada on the grounds of being a conscientious objector. He had been influenced by certain Muslim teachings on conscientious objection. Then, while studying at a university in the US, he happened to have a Mennonite roommate. Their discussions led him to deepen his conscientious objector commitment. Turkey, however, had no legal provisions for conscientious objection. People who refused to serve in the military were given two-year prison sentences which were re-imposed again and again if the individuals persisted in refusing to serve.

This young man had obtained a student visa to study in the US but that could not be extended. Not wanting to return to Turkey, he decided to come to Canada and ask for refugee status. He had appeared before the IRB but it refused him; so too had the Federal Court. Their reasoning was that to be prosecuted for refusing to serve in the military did not constitute persecution as defined by the UN Convention for Refugees, and that the law requiring military service was "of general application" and could therefore not be said to violate any one person's rights.

After these refusals, the only avenue left was that of appealing to the Minister. This young man had a legal-aid lawyer but he came to our office and asked for help. I then contacted the lawyer and learned about his line of argumentation; we agreed that I would prepare a supplementary letter to the Minister who, at that time, was

Monte Solberg. In our letter I reviewed the history of conscientious objector laws in Canada dating back to 1793, and the experience of Canadian COs in the two world wars. Then I described the post WW II trend in western countries to accept conscientious objection as a "right," referring to formal steps taken by the European Parliament and the United Nations Commission for Human Rights and to changes in the International Covenant on Civil and Political Rights. I also referred to the Canadian Charter of Rights and Freedoms and to a 1981 letter (mentioned in the story about constitutional reform below) from the then Justice Minister, Jean Chrétien, which held that the Charter's freedom of conscience provision was sufficiently broad to cover conscientious objection.

Interestingly, in the fall of 2007, while we were still waiting for a response from the Minister, the Parliamentary Committee on Immigration and Citizenship held hearings on American "deserters," meaning people who had been in the US military but who, determined not to serve in Iraq, had fled to Canada. These hearings gave us an opportunity to present a brief to the Committee outlining the history of conscientious objector provisions and their more recent development. I stated: "... historically, the Mennonite people have benefitted very substantially from Canada's conscientious objector provisions. We want others to be able to benefit from similar protections." I then took the opportunity to also describe the situation of this man from Turkey.

Not long thereafter, this man received a notice asking him to come to a particular government office to pick up an envelope containing the Minister's decision. Having shared his anxiety with us over the preceding months, he now asked me to go with him. I will never forget his relief when we read the letter and learned that he would be allowed to stay. The letter also suggested that our submission had been significant in the decision. Not long thereafter, that young man enrolled in law school and went on to become a lawyer in the Canadian government.

4

FOREIGN POLICY, DEVELOPMENT, AND PEACE

◆

A large portion of our advocacy work dealt with foreign policy issues. This is to be expected, given that a majority of MCC's work was devoted to overseas needs. The situations which we in Ottawa addressed, whether by letters, personal meetings, or through coalitions, included conflicts in Mozambique, Malawi, Sudan, Ethiopia, Angola, Central America, Colombia, and other places, as well as cruise missile testing, land mines, nuclear disarmament, major defence equipment purchases, the Strategic Defense Initiative, etc. I will recount six general submissions.

Foreign Policy as a Whole, 1985
In 1985 the new Mulroney government mandated a Parliamentary Committee to hold public hearings to seek input for a new foreign policy. The plan to hold hearings was an open door for groups like MCC. Mennonite churches had never yet spoken on our country's foreign policy in a comprehensive way. Not to try it, given this opportunity, seemed wrong.

After consulting extensively with colleagues in MCC and with various church leaders, I prepared a 15-page brief entitled, "The Well-Being of All". It began with a Biblical quotation:

> It shall come to pass in the latter days
> that ... they shall beat their swords into ploughshares
> and their spears into pruning hooks;
> nation shall not lift up sword against nation,
> neither shall they learn war anymore;
> but they shall sit every man under his vine and under his
>   fig tree,
> and none shall make them afraid;
> for the mouth of the Lord of hosts has spoken.
>   Micah 4: 1-4 (RSV)

We then explained:

> We come not with theoretical expertise but with a fraternity of relations with people in a broad range of countries. These relations stem from: our international development programs with about 900 volunteers in some 50 countries; the historic migrations of some Mennonites, with the result that there are about 50,000 in Russia even today and sizeable numbers also in several Latin American countries; and the century of Mennonite and Brethren in Christ missionary work contributing to the fact of sister churches in about 60 countries....We have asked ourselves, what might these partners abroad say if they were asked about Canada's foreign policy?

Our two main themes were international development and militarism. On the former we said, with regard to people in poorer countries, that:

> Farmers see the prices of their produce kept low or falling ... while the cost of fuel and other inputs has risen. Roads to get produce to markets are neglected as governments use money for other purposes. Few have access to easy credit. Employment prospects fade with the decline in world demand for third world commodities and with the erection by developed countries of barriers against

the importation of third world manufactured products ... land that should be used to produce locally needed food is used to grow export crops in order to earn foreign exchange to service debts ...

We called for Canada to increase its aid to its oft-stated target of 0.7% of GNP and to "untie" more of it, meaning that recipient countries would be freer to decide on where to buy what they needed, rather than being required to spend most of it on Canadian goods and services. Regarding the crushing debt load of many poor countries, we said that often this was the result of factors outside their control, such as increases in international interest rates or a drop in the prices for their products. Further, in many countries the cost of servicing the debt had become such that far more money flowed from poor countries to richer ones than the other way around, and that poor countries were "under great pressure to orient their productive capacity ... toward exports in order to earn foreign exchange" rather than for their own food security and development.

On militarism, we affirmed Canada's longstanding efforts to promote understanding between the US and the USSR; we encouraged work for a nuclear test ban, for a prohibition of chemical weapons, for strengthening the nuclear non-proliferation treaty, and for a pull-back from the trend toward weapons with an "aggressive posture," meaning weapons that have not only a retaliatory capacity but a capability to threaten and to carry out a limited nuclear war. We also called for particular actions in the Middle East, Southeast Asia, and Central America. Finally, we emphasized the importance of people-to-people exchanges, assisting refugees, and broad family reunification provisions in immigration, referring to Mennonites in the Soviet Union.

Our brief was approved by MCCC's Executive Committee on November 29, 1985, although we did not appear before the Parliamentary Committee until April 24, 1986. For that we decided to focus on Southeast Asia, knowing that other groups would not address that situation. To help present our views I was joined by Larry Kehler and Stuart Clark, two MCCers who had had a considerable on-the-ground involvement there, as well as by J. M. Klassen, the Executive Director of MCCC.

In addition to that in-person appearance, I sent copies of the written submission to a range of people, some of whom sent noteworthy responses. Senator Heath MacQuarrie wrote:

> As I would expect the views of the M.C.C. reveal a compassionate concern underlaid with thoughtful and informed understanding ... I find the totality ... a splendid document.

Geoffrey Pearson, who at that time was the Executive Director of the Canadian Institute for International Peace and Security but had previously served as Ambassador to the Soviet Union, said this:

> It reflects some of the most humanitarian thoughts on international issues ... I have circulated it to my staff for their consideration.

The office of the Rt. Hon. Joe Clark, Minister for External Affairs, wrote:

> There is no doubt that the thoughtful and comprehensive remarks contained in the Mennonite Central Committee's document will constitute a useful contribution to the ongoing foreign policy review. Allow me, on Mr. Clark's behalf, to congratulate you and your colleagues for this important and fine piece of analysis.

Such responses suggest that our brief may have had an effect on the thinking of some people, perhaps to reinforce certain perspectives, but it must also be acknowledged that some of our points were not unique to us. Other groups made similar ones.

Foreign Aid, 1986
Soon after that review of Canada's overall foreign policy, the Mulroney government launched a review of CIDA policy specifically,

CIDA being the Canadian International Development Agency. I looked forward to preparing a brief on this. I assumed that MCC's vast experience in international development work would enable us to give a lot of good advice to the government. I then made a point at one MCC meeting to have dinner with a number of senior MCCers and to probe their thinking. The result was disappointing. I concluded that many of the ideas that MCC tried to follow in its own development work were not easily applied to the government's framework.

Despite that disappointment, I wrote up a submission, calling it "Thy Neighbour's Keeper." In it I reviewed MCC's development work and expressed gratitude for the funding we received from CIDA and for the non-political character of that funding. Then we asked that the prohibition on using CIDA money in Vietnam and Cambodia be lifted, that the CIDA budget generally be increased, and that the percentage of it that was tied to the purchase of Canadian products be reduced. We emphasized the importance of supporting multilateral organizations like the United Nations High Commissioner for Refugees, the World Food Programme and the Food and Agriculture Organization; we cautioned against using CIDA money for promoting business, although we acknowledged that business and investment were important for third-world development; we restated our concern about the debt burden of many poor countries but also commended the government for certain positive steps on this matter; we cautioned against making all aid conditional on a country's respect for human rights lest that serve to further punish those most in need; and we also called for initiatives to promote peace in Central America, in Southeast Asia, and in several conflicts in Africa.

Bert Lobe and Stuart Clark from the MCCC Overseas Services office of MCCC joined me in appearing before the committee on October 29, 1986. Once again we talked quite a lot about Vietnam and Cambodia and the need for changes in Canadian policy toward that region.

Defence, 1989

In 1987, the Mulroney government issued a White Paper on defence. This meant that non-governmental groups could now submit responses. Project Ploughshares, where I served on the board, prepared an elaborate response on behalf of its member churches. MCC was a member of Ploughshares, indeed a founding member, and MCC was pleased with most of the Ploughshares paper, but there was uneasiness, particularly among MCC staff, about the fact that Ploughshares explicitly allowed that in some rare situations it might be legitimate for the state to use a certain limited force in the defence of peace and justice. Most of the churches in Ploughshares supported that view.

Within MCC, the question of whether to endorse the Ploughshares submission received considerable discussion. In the end, the board concluded that it would not do that; instead, we could prepare a submission of our own, which I was then asked to write. The resulting 1,500-word letter, dated March 28, 1989, was addressed to the Prime Minister. In it we referred to the historic Mennonite conscientious objector stance, to the way Mennonite people had experienced the destruction of war, especially in the two world wars, and to how MCC's ongoing international work provided far too many reminders of the destructive results of war.

We then addressed defence and security concerns in relation to both east-west tensions and "third world" situations. Regarding the former, we noted recent positive developments and called for additional steps, including stopping the weaponization of space and the testing of nuclear warheads and their delivery systems; as well, we urged the government to press NATO to back away from what seemed like a provocative stance and to reduce the size of its forces. Regarding the third world, we urged the government to reduce Canada's export of military goods and to press for an international regime to curb the flow of weapons in general and instead to do more to promote economic justice. We said that the lack of economic justice led to popular uprisings, which were then suppressed by governments who, in order to do that, needed to

Foreign Policy, Development, and Peace 45

spend what money they had to purchase weapons.

I sent copies of the letter to some 70 MPs. A good number of them responded warmly. Ray Funk, then an MP from Saskatchewan, wrote: "This is an excellent letter, both in content and craftsmanship." Lloyd Axworthy, then an Opposition MP, wrote, "Be assured that I will do what I can to hold them (the government) to the high standards that you have set." But was our letter was really different from the Ploughshares paper? Admittedly, nowhere did our letter say, explicitly, that the use of force might ever be legitimate but neither did we argue that the government should never use it.

When I prepared this letter, I shared a draft with a Jewish friend who was very knowledgeable about defence issues. He spoke positively of the technical and strategic parts but felt that something was missing. He felt that when people see a major letter from MCC on defence, they expect an articulation of the moral dimensions of peace and security. What a helpful reminder! I had been preoccupied with the technical parts.

Canada's Arms Trade, 1992

In April 1992, the Standing Committee on External Affairs and International Trade authorized a subcommittee to hold hearings on Canada's arms exports. Canada allowed arms manufacturers to export their goods because they were legal businesses and because for a country to have arms for self-defence purposes was seen as legitimate and necessary for stability in the international order. However, there were regulations to control exports, particularly to countries that were involved in hostilities, or were about to be so involved, or had a record of violating the human rights of their citizens.

In making our critique, we relied heavily on the research and arguments of Project Ploughshares. We said that in reality the policy restraints were too weak, and that to make them effective, there should be a review mechanism, preferably by a Parliamentary Committee, that could receive public input. We also proposed that before approving arms exports, there should be a Security Impact Assessment somewhat like Environmental Assessments that are done before pipelines and other infrastructure projects get approved. Further, we challenged the view that governmental grants given to arms industries were an effective way to create jobs.

My colleague, Ed Epp, then working in the MCCC office in Winnipeg, joined me in presenting this brief. Having recently completed five years of MCC service in the Middle East, he could recount first-hand stories about the effects of the massive inflow of weapons to that region. We also had reports from MCC workers in other parts of the world. "In summary," we said, "our view is that arms exports do not contribute to peace and justice." A few years later, the regulations were tightened somewhat.

A 2001 Submission Derailed

In 2001, the government of Jean Chrétien authorized a ministerial review of CIDA. We, like other NGOs, looked forward to this. In the mid-1990s there had been substantial cuts in the CIDA budget, but now there was hope for increases and a general renewal. The Minister, Maria Minna, planned to lead a cross-Canada consultation on a discussion paper entitled "Strengthening Aid Effectiveness: New Approaches for Canada's International Assistance Program." Our written submission was dated September 10, and we were scheduled to appear before her team on September 20.

In our 1,600 word submission, we called for "a stronger commitment to poverty reduction" given that, by the government's own admission, "1.5 billion people ... now live in absolute poverty on less than US $1 per day." We also called for "careful attention to local circumstances" in developing poverty reduction strategies and to support the development of "human capital through education, redistributing productive assets such as credit and land." Further, noting that in total far more money flowed from poor countries to rich countries than the other way around, we urged the government to ensure that its policies in the areas of trade, finance, the environment, and other areas supported its aid objectives and did not undermine them. We also called for a commitment to peacebuilding, conflict resolution and human security.

Our submission addressed important areas, but before we got to present it the world changed. The horrific attacks on the World Trade Towers in New York took place on September 11. Thus, on September 20, we were received politely but it was clear that the mind of the government was elsewhere. Security and the threat of terrorism had become overriding concerns.

Foreign Policy, 2005
Paul Martin became Prime Minister in 2003. He was eager to develop new policies in a number of areas. To formulate a new foreign policy, he asked a Parliamentary Committee to hold hearings. Again, MCC asked me to prepare a brief. We called it "Promoting Development and Building Peace," implying that we saw these two as paramount goals for Canada. On October 31, 2005, Don Peters, the Executive Director of MCCC, and I presented this 3,500 word brief to the Committee.

We referred to the 1994 genocide in Rwanda to illustrate the issues. We noted, among other things, that in 1990 the World Bank had imposed a structural adjustment program that had devalued that country's currency by 80% and that the collapse of the International Coffee Agreement had reduced the value of its main export by half. These and other traumatic developments, over which Rwanda had no control, had devastated the economy and this in turn had exacerbated the inter-ethnic tensions that then broke out in the genocide, claiming 800,000 lives. We then argued that Canada should look at all of its tools, including aid, debt relief, trade, human rights work and its involvement in multilateral bodies like the World Bank and the UN, in order to promote development and build peace in vulnerable societies.

More specifically, we argued for: (i) increased aid and better coordination among donor countries so that recipient countries would know what they could count on; (ii) debt relief, noting that because of changes in international interest rates, many poor countries had already paid back far, far more than they had ever borrowed; and (iii) fairness in trade, noting that too often poor countries were pressured to open their markets to heavily subsidized agricultural products from richer countries while the international prices for the products of poor countries, like coffee or cotton, were not protected.

On peacebuilding, we urged the government to work for nuclear disarmament, particularly in relation to the Nuclear Non-Proliferation Agreement, which Canada had helped to formulate in the 1960s, and to work for substantial international restrictions on the trade in small arms which, we said, claimed half a million lives per year. We endorsed the principle of human security as opposed to security only for states. We also called for extensive diplomatic work to address conflict situations, climate change, and human rights, particularly those of women and refugees.

In conclusion we said that "Our concerns ... arise from our faith that God wants the well-being of the world and of all people in it; further, that there is a calling for individuals, church organizations, citizens groups, and governments, despite different roles, to contribute to that well-being."

Less than one month after we presented that brief to the Parliamentary Committee, Paul Martin's government, which was in a minority situation, was defeated in the House of Commons. That led to the election of January 23, 2006 in which Stephen Harper became Prime Minister. His government did not hold a public review of foreign policy issues in my remaining time with MCC.

5

VIETNAM AND CAMBODIA

◆

From the late 1970s until the 1990s, we did a lot of advocacy work in relation to Vietnam and Cambodia. As noted in the refugee stories earlier, MCC had started doing relief work in Vietnam in 1954. That was when France's war to regain control of Indochina (Vietnam, Cambodia, and Laos) ended in failure. It was also when Vietnam was divided into North and South. This 'temporary' division was to be resolved through general elections in 1956. But in 1955 leaders of the South declared it to be a separate country. With that, US support of South Vietnam increased, seeing it threatened by the communist North which, in turn, was supported by the bigger communist powers of China and the USSR. But in 1975, this US effort also ended in failure, despite enormous death and destruction. (US bombing on those countries during these years exceeded its bombing in all areas during World War II.)

The initial stance of the Canadian government toward the new Vietnam was somewhat sympathetic. Having established formal diplomatic relations with North Vietnam in 1973, Canada extended that recognition to the government of the united Vietnam in 1975. It was not a wholehearted embrace; after all, Vietnam was strongly supported by the Soviet Union. But Canada and other western countries did provide a significant amount of humanitarian and reconstruction assistance to Vietnam in those early years. It was not long, however, before circumstances changed and Canada's stance took a different turn. That meant that the context and focus of our advocacy work also changed. I will recount the story in four sections.

Trying to Build Relations, 1975 – 1979
As with other areas of conflict, we invited returning MCC workers to meet with officials and MPs. James Klassen was one of several MCCers who, after the fall of South Vietnam, had continued to work there for a number of months even when virtually all other westerners left. Thus he was able to describe the situation, the massive social uprooting and dislocation during the war, the consequences of the sudden end of the large American presence, and the need for assistance. On questions of religious freedom James remained somewhat hopeful despite the ideology of the new regime.

We also invited Murray and Linda Hiebert, who had served in Vietnam too. They discussed the food aid needs and asked about technology to detect and destroy unexploded ordnances that were causing countless injuries to farmers as they worked their fields. Would Canada have such technology from its own military test ranges? MP Jake Epp inquired of the Defence Department, and we did some follow up work but concluded that the technology used here by Canada's forces was not suitable for Vietnam. MCC, however, found other devices, namely rototillers, and sent a good number of them to Vietnam.

What stands out most from these early years relates to the Vietnamese Embassy in Ottawa. Vietnam wanted to receive aid but it did not allow western aid workers to live there. MCC then decided to ship relief supplies, followed up by delegations to check on their end use and to build relations. Since the US did not allow Vietnam to have an embassy there—indeed, the US had an embargo on trade, aid, and other interaction with Vietnam—it fell to us in Ottawa to arrange the relief shipments and the visits. A key person at the Embassy was a Mr. Luong Manh Tuan. He always received

Vietnam and Cambodia

us warmly and was eager to move things forward. One time when John Wieler, Overseas Services director for MCC in Winnipeg, had returned from a visit to Vietnam and was in Ottawa for CIDA meetings, Mr. Tuan arranged a special dinner for us at the Embassy to celebrate MCC-Vietnam relations. Later, when my colleague, Robert Koop, married Deborah Martin in Quebec, he came out to the wedding and interacted eagerly with various guests.

In 1979, however, we had to have some difficult conversations. In December of 1978, Vietnam invaded Cambodia, overthrew the Khmer Rouge (KR) regime, and set up a new government led by a KR defector, Hang Samrin. Vietnam argued that the KR regime had been genocidal and that it had made a number of military forays into Vietnamese territory. Nevertheless, Vietnam's invasion was seen as a violation of international law, so western countries who had shown some sympathy towards Vietnam now pulled away. Thus, the Canadian government stopped its aid program. Also at this time, thousands of "boat people" from Vietnam were starting to arrive in Canada. As noted in the refugee stories, Mennonite churches were at the forefront of sponsoring and resettling these refugees. They were telling heart-rending accounts of the harshness of Vietnam's new government, including its practice of sending people to re-education camps. We wanted Mr. Tuan to understand that these developments were of deep concern to MCC and its supporting churches.

On one occasion in the fall of 1979 we discussed these issues forthrightly at a hurriedly arranged dinner in a side room at a downtown restaurant. John Wieler was in Ottawa for meetings again. And John Reimer, a newly elected Member of Parliament, was interested in our work. So we called Mr. Tuan, who then came with several colleagues from the Embassy. Of course he defended his government, pointing out that the KR government had killed a quarter of the Cambodian people and had attacked Vietnam repeatedly and claimed a sizeable chunk of its territory. Mr. Tuan was impressive as he told Vietnam's side of the story, but the western world was turning away. Vietnam was no longer looked upon primarily as a victim. Before long Vietnam closed its Embassy in Ottawa. With that, our role in negotiating visits and relief shipments ended.

Facing Closed Doors, 1979 – 1986
Vietnam's invasion of Cambodia led to a complex international configuration that was aimed at, among other things, isolating Vietnam. But it did not happen immediately. At first, in 1979, western countries provided substantial amounts of aid to Cambodia, now called Kampuchea. They had been aware of the plight of the Cambodian people under KR rule. Now they wanted to provide them with at least some support. But by early 1980 that initial helpfulness ended. One reason related to the interests and machinations of the super powers: the US, the USSR, and China. China had long supported the KR while Vietnam was aligned with the Soviet Union. Also, there was an old border dispute between Vietnam and China. Thus, in 1979, China briefly invaded Vietnam, saying it wanted to "teach Vietnam a lesson." By continuing to support the KR resistance to the new government in Cambodia, China could "bleed Vietnam" as one journalist put it. The United States was also against Vietnam for many reasons including that Vietnam's patron, the Soviet Union, was its global rival in the Cold War, and it, incidentally, had just invaded Afghanistan. Some countries in the region such as Thailand, Indonesia, and Malaysia also had concerns and interests, and may have welcomed a stronger alignment with the US.

Thus, in 1980 Canada and other western countries stopped virtually all of their assistance for people under the new government in Phnom Penh, Cambodia. At the same time, they provided considerable aid for the estimated 300,000 Cambodians who had gone to the Thai border when Vietnam invaded. These people on the border were referred to as refugees, but it was widely believed that many had been compelled to go there by the retreating forces, either those of the KR or those of two small non-communist resistance groups. To facilitate the flow of aid to these border groups, the UN set up the Border Relief Organization (UNBRO). Though small, these groups would have a particular role in the unfolding political drama. By 1982 the two non-communist groups were persuaded to join with the KR in forming the Coalition Government of Democratic Kampuchea (CGDK) of which the legendary Prince Sihanouk became the titular head. Western countries now recognized and supported the CGDK; they could say that they were supporting an alternative to the new Phnom Penh government but not supporting the KR, at least not directly.

Meanwhile, the KR, from its camps on the Thai border and with Chinese support, launched periodic attacks on the territory held by the Vietnamese-imposed government in Phnom Penh. So did the smaller non-communist groups, with US support, though to a lesser extent. Clearly, Vietnam and the Phnom Penh government were being pressed hard. Canada did not provide military support for the CGDK but did support this general orientation. In July 1980, when Canada's External Affairs minister, Mark MacGuigan, returned from an ASEAN* meeting, he described Vietnam as having become a "brutal, imperialistic power" and said that, supported by the Soviet Union, it was a threat to the region.

How was MCC to work in this context? How could we provide relief for the people and work for peace? We had no desire to defend either the government of Vietnam, or the one in Phnom Penh, but it seemed important to challenge some of the prevailing views and to remember the enormous destruction that the people there had suffered at the hands of western powers. Larry Kehler, who had just returned from an MCC assignment in the region when he read MacGuigan's comments, responded with a long letter. Having been inside Cambodia, he said that the people clearly preferred the new government of Hang Samrin to that of the KR, that now they were able to "till the soil" and "get the rice crop in" and begin to "put their lives together again." He sharply refuted the claim of officials in the

---

* ASEAN stands for Association of Southeast Asian Nations. It included Thailand, Malaysia, Indonesia, the Philippines, and a few others.

Canadian Embassy in Bangkok who had told him that Cambodia was in chaos and that there was no progress in getting people back on their feet. He told MacGuigan, "Your stance looks very much like that of China and the United States. I am dismayed that we Canadians are allowing ourselves to be pushed into such a patently inhumane and immoral position."

Over the next several years we made a number of appeals. We asked for permission to use CIDA money for our relief work in these countries; we also urged the government to support the Red Cross, the WFP, and other multilateral bodies. Bert Lobe, MCC's Asia Secretary who travelled to the region on a regular basis, came to Ottawa several times to describe the situation on the ground. We also brought in Murray Hiebert who, though a Canadian, was now working on these issues in Washington, as well as Nancy Pocock, a prominent Quaker, and various others. Of course when MCC workers on the field were on home leave we brought them in to talk about what they were hearing and seeing. Louise and Jake Buhler, from Saskatchewan, who served in the region for 20 years, were particularly helpful. We were not uncritical about Vietnam. Its approach to human rights and religious freedom were of concern to us. Its ideology certainly hindered development but, we felt, this did not warrant the country's isolation.

Twice I tried to persuade MPs to join in a Parliamentary delegation to visit the region and learn about the situation first hand. MPs had made such visits to the Middle East, Latin America, and elsewhere. I wrote up detailed proposals for such visits, but there was not enough interest. Vietnam's announcement in 1985 that it would withdraw its forces from Cambodia by 1990 was given little credibility. In April 1986 when we appeared before the Parliamentary Committee on Foreign Affairs, we used our allotted speaking time to focus on Vietnam and Cambodia. In May of that year I was part of an MCC-arranged interchurch delegation to the region. This led to more meetings with officials and MPs. But the doors of the Canadian government seemed to be closed. On the matter of aid, the government's position was that "Vietnam's continued occupation of Kampuchea and the diversion of its resources to military pursuits beyond its borders" precluded the provision of Canadian governmental assistance.

An incident in May 1983 revealed a particular angle of the negative views toward Vietnam. By this time MCC had sent a number of delegations to Vietnam but felt that there would also be value in having a delegation of Vietnamese visit Canada. Four men came. They visited Mennonite churches and communities, but I had asked that their itinerary include Ottawa as well. When I then contacted External Affairs officials and MPs about meeting with them, I found that the doors did not open easily, although Lloyd Axworthy, then Minister of Immigration, did receive them.

I also wanted these Vietnamese guests to meet Canadian NGO representatives. For this I planned a noonhour meeting and reserved a room in a downtown church. But when the time came and these visitors and I walked toward the church, we saw a crowd of placard-waving local Vietnamese loudly denouncing the government of Vietnam. I was shocked. I had meant for this to be a by-invitation-only event but one person, whom I had trusted, had spread the word. Upon seeing the crowd, our guests quickly retreated to the safety of their hotel, the Lord Elgin, while I tried to talk to the demonstrators. Many of these protesting Vietnamese had only recently come as refugees. They spoke about the harsh oppression of the communist government in Vietnam.

I explained to the protesters that MCC was at the forefront of bringing Vietnamese refugees to Canada but also wanted to have Vietnamese representatives learn about us and about Canada. My pleas were in vain. The meeting with NGO representatives could not take place. In the following weeks I met with leaders of the protesting group. They then prepared a thoughtful three-page letter which I could share with MCC colleagues. They outlined the suffering of the Vietnamese people under the new government and the kind of assistance that MCC should try to provide. They said the new authorities in Vietnam were "more interested in their imperialist wars against their neighbours (Laos, Kampuchea, and recently Thailand) than in relieving the suffrances of their own people." We agreed that the Vietnamese government was oppressive but felt that some involvement should nevertheless by pursued.

Even though we were not allowed to use CIDA money, Canada, unlike the US, did not prevent groups like MCC from providing aid in these countries if we used our own church funds. Indeed, several of the letters from External Affairs ministers, while refusing to let us use government funding, seemed to commend us for continuing to work there. Then, in 1987, there was a positive step on the aid question: the Parliamentary committee studying Canada's foreign aid policy recommended that NGOs be allowed to use CIDA money for their work in these countries. MP John Reimer, a member of that committee, had pressed for that. Unfortunately, it would be another two-and-a-half years before the government accepted that recommendation. But our aim was not only to access CIDA money; it was for Canada to become politically engaged so as to help overcome the impasse that isolated Vietnam and Cambodia from the West and contributed so much to the suffering of the people.

Supporting Steps Toward a Political Solution, 1987 – 1990
By 1987, there were signs that the broader political situation might change. Soviet leaders indicated that they would not support Vietnam indefinitely; they began to talk with China about Cambodia. Indonesia, a prominent member of ASEAN, began to talk with Vietnam about steps toward a resolution. And Prince Norodom Sihanouk, who had ruled Cambodia during the "golden years" before 1968 but was now with the CGDK, met with Hun Sen, who had replaced Hang Samrin as head of the Phnom Penh government. Hun Sen hoped that Sihanouk would join his government and bring with him the coveted international legitimacy which could end Cambodia's isolation and perhaps enable his government to access western aid sources like the World Bank. However, Sihanouk was not willing to go that far.

Another key development was Vietnam's announcement in May 1988 that it would withdraw half of its forces by the end of that year and the rest in 1989. This opened a major question: Would that result in a vacuum and would the KR move into that vacuum and regain power? If it would, that would be extremely unfortunate. Vietnam requested that its withdrawal be monitored and verified, so that the international community would know that it was happening and then accept responsibility for the resulting situation in Cambodia. Indeed, Vietnam asked specifically for Canada's involvement in such a monitoring mission, claiming that Canada's word might be accepted by both the US and China. Canada's response, however, was one of caution, as was that of ASEAN. I tried to persuade Canadian officials and MPs to become involved in the monitoring mission, but in a July 1988 meeting I was told me that Canada was not convinced that Vietnam was serious about withdrawing.

For us there was another development. A group of NGOs, including large church bodies from Europe and the US, among them MCC, had formed "The NGO Forum on Kampuchea." One of the Forum's projects was the book, *Punishing the Poor: The International Isolation of Kampuchea*, released on January 1, 1988. Now the Forum retained Raoul Jennar, a retired Belgian diplomat, for a "shuttle diplomacy" assignment. He would travel to the region and meet with senior government representatives in Phnom Penh and in some ASEAN capitals, and then to travel to western capitals to discuss possible new initiatives. In the spring of 1989, I hosted him in Ottawa. He strongly challenged Canadian officials on their general view and also on the importance of monitoring and verifying Vietnam's withdrawal, believing that that would cause the US to take seriously the possibility of a KR return and to take preventive measures.

The possibility of the KR returning prompted other steps. In June 1989 we in MCC wrote this to External Affairs Minister Joe Clark:

> ... [W]hat will happen after September when Vietnam's forces are to be completely withdrawn; will there be a long civil war; will the Khmer Rouge armed forces

overthrow the Hun Sen government; will there be another genocidal rule? ... a number of actions are needed. The withdrawal of the Vietnamese forces needs to be confirmed in an internationally credible way. The Khmer Rouge dominated coalition should not be recognized as the legitimate representative of Cambodia at the UN. The United States and China, who in different ways seem to be calling for a substantial involvement of Khmer Rouge forces in an interim government, need to be persuaded to stop doing so. There needs to be assistance in various procedural matters so that democratic elections can be held. Also needed is economic development aid.

Reg Reimer, a long time missionary in Vietnam and now head of World Relief Canada, made a similar plea, as did Professor David Wurfel on behalf of the United Church. The Canadian Council for International Cooperation (CCIC), an NGO umbrella organization, hosted a conference on Cambodia in May 1989. Also around this time I happened to sit beside a key adviser to Minister Clark at a government dinner. We had a lengthy and fruitful discussion.

Given the signs of change, there was considerable international discussion about the need for a comprehensive settlement, one that would involve the Phnom Penh government, the three resistance groups, and all their various international supporters. Presumably, such a settlement would lead to a reformulation of the government in Phnom Penh and provide it with international legitimacy. Thus, in July 1989, France convened a peace conference on Cambodia. Canada participated, but the conference was widely seen as a failure, in part because the participants did not agree on a way to include the KR in a power sharing arrangement while also making sure that the KR could not regain power. The failure to get a settlement was serious, because a number of western countries insisted on such a settlement before they would provide resources and become involved. But the absence of outside involvement increased the chances that, with Vietnam's withdrawal, the KR would make their way back and regain control of the country. In the fall of 1989, an MCC worker in Phnom Penh wrote, "the Khmers are feeling pessimistic and fearful about the future ... because the Khmer Rouge ..."

Fortunately, not everyone waited for a comprehensive agreement before taking further steps. Several ASEAN countries, including Thailand, were in direct discussions with Vietnam and with representatives of the government in Phnom Penh. And in Canada, Joe Clark hosted a roundtable on Cambodia in December 1989. The two dozen participants included several academics, CIDA and External Affairs officials, a Red Cross worker just back from Cambodia, several Cambodian and Vietnamese Canadians, and a few NGO representatives including us from MCC. Part of the discussion was about whether Canada could, and should, become more involved and provide aid even before a comprehensive settlement was reached. Those of us from NGOs argued that the needs were great and that it was possible to work there effectively.

A few weeks later, in January 1990, I participated in a CCIC organized trip to Cambodia, together with four other Canadian NGO representatives. We were joined by an official from the Canadian Embassy in Bangkok. This indicated that the Canadian government was thinking of further steps. Our delegation reported that the events of the preceding decades, the US bombing, the civil war, the KR rule, and the isolation throughout the 1980s had left the people in a dire situation. We said that western NGOs were able to work there, that their work was effective, that CIDA funding should be made available, and that these steps did not need to wait for a political settlement, however valuable that would be.

On January 25, 1990, while we were still on our trip, Joe Clark announced a new policy. Now, NGOs working in Vietnam, Laos, and Cambodia would be allowed to use CIDA funds. Clark also acknowledged that

> ... the current regime in Phnom Penh is more than

simply one of four factions … it appears to have provided adequate government and its record in most areas is far better than that of the Khmer Rouge Government which preceded it. Nowhere is this more evident than in the field of human rights and in basic respect for human life.

The wording was diplomatic but it reflected a significant change in policy. More than other western countries, Canada was now acknowledging the Hun Sen government in Phnom Penh. And regarding aid, CIDA's bilateral division now invited MCC and a few other NGOs to form a coalition, funded by CIDA, to do development work in Cambodia. In addition to providing economic assistance, this would represent a positive diplomatic overture toward the Hun Sen government in Phnom Penh. This was a major step. Before long we had more than a dozen NGOs, including small Cambodian Canadian groups, on board. We then formed the "Cambodia Canada Development Program" (CCDP), hired staff and soon had a substantial Canadian aid program on the ground in Cambodia. The CCDP also had an Advocacy Committee which I chaired. In this capacity I participated in The NGO Forum On Kampuchea, hosted Raoul Jennar several more times, and interacted frequently with External Affairs and CIDA officials who were now more like partners than adversaries.

Seeking Peace Amid a Conflicted Process, 1990 – 1993
Even though Canada had now taken significant steps, there was still no comprehensive settlement. But there were ongoing discussions. When the Paris conference of July 1989 failed, the Permanent Five on the UN Security Council (the Soviet Union, China, the US, Britain, and France) had begun to work on a Framework Document. It was released in August 1990. It was only a framework; it lacked detail on key questions, including questions about the KR. Over the next year there were further discussions in Paris, Jakarta, Tokyo, and Thailand, etc.

Then on October 23, 1991, in Paris, a full agreement (actually

Vietnam and Cambodia

three agreements) was signed. It was massive in scope and there were serious questions. It called on the UN to monitor a cease-fire, facilitate a substantial dismantling of the different parties' armed forces, prepare and conduct elections, supervise several departments of the Phnom Penh government so that they did not interfere in the elections, repatriate the 300,000 people who had spent the preceding decade in camps at the Thai-Cambodian border, set up a program for the country's reconstruction, etc. Could all this be done? Would the KR respect the agreement and the other parties in it? Would the world cover the estimated $1.8 billion cost and provide the projected 20,000 personnel? An additional factor was that the government in Phnom Penh, which was still serving 95% of the people, had lost much of its funding when the Soviet Union collapsed. It desperately needed financial support.

Soon after the agreement was signed there were moves to cut it back. This prompted NGOs in a number of countries to appeal to their governments. In May 1992, we wrote to Canada's External Affairs Minister, Barbara McDougall, saying:

> ... [If] that multifaceted [peace] process is to be even moderately successful then there will have to be strong and sustained international support. We are writing to ask that Canada provide this kind of support and that it press other countries to do so too.... the $680 million that Canada reportedly provided for the Gulf War leads us to believe that Canada can also make a very substantial contribution to Cambodia.

I wrote several articles in newspapers, describing the precarious situation and urging the government to provide the needed support and work with other countries to address key issues. Late in May 1992, we in the CCDP organized a conference on Parliament Hill and obtained the co-sponsorship of an MP from each party, (Walter McLean, Christine Stewart, and Svend Robinson). It was well-attended by government officials, academics, Cambodian Canadians, retired diplomats like Geoffrey Pearson, and others. For a keynote speaker, we were able to get Dith Pran, the Cambodian journalist whose experience was at the centre of the highly acclaimed movie, "The Killing Fields." (After his speech, I wanted to give him the $1,000 in cash that we had agreed on. But the only private corner that was available to count out the money was a small men's washroom. Both of us found that quite amusing.)

The Cambodian settlement was very imperfect. So too was the Hun Sen government which won the elections and thus gained international legitimacy. The demobilization of fighters and the demining of agricultural lands and the resettling of displaced people, and various other things were not carried out as well as had been planned. But the long impasse had been broken; the isolation was ended; and new possibilities were opened. And Canada had played a significant role. Perhaps the easing of the Cold War had given Canada a freer hand. In any case, Canadian officials, at the direction of Minister Joe Clark, worked hard to move things forward, well ahead of the US and other western governments. And MCC, both from the field and in Ottawa, had helped. We had long been the main Canadian NGO talking about the Cambodian situation and calling for a better policy.

6

PALESTINE AND ISRAEL

◆

Before World War I (1914-1918), most of the Middle East was under the Ottoman Empire. By 1917, the British anticipated that they would emerge victorious and as a result gain control of large parts of the Middle East, including Palestine. At that point, and in response to the Zionist movement that had taken shape in Europe in the last part of the 19th century, Britain issued what became known as the Balfour declaration. With this, Britain promised to establish "a national home for the Jewish people," without doing anything that might "prejudice the civil and religious rights of existing non-Jewish communities in Palestine."

After that war, the newly created League of Nations gave Britain a "mandate" to control Palestine as a temporary trusteeship for the stated purpose of facilitating its development. "Mandate Palestine" was defined as the area from the Jordan River to the Mediterranean Sea. A 1920 British government report estimated that there were 700,000 people then living in Palestine, that most of these were Arab Muslims but that 77,000 were Arab Christians, and that 76,000 were Jewish people. Most of the latter were said to have moved to Palestine in the preceding forty years due to the violent pogroms in Eastern Europe. Many more Jewish people would come in the next twenty years. Often they acquired land by purchasing it from absentee landlords.

Many Arab people, both Muslim and Christian, felt that the

term "mandate" was just a new word for "colony." They wanted independence just as people in Africa and Asia wanted independence from colonial rule. Palestinian Arabs envisioned a pluralistic state with firm protections for minority groups, including the Jewish people. However, some Jewish leaders—those in Palestine and those in the Western countries—pressed for a sovereign Jewish state. This became known as the Zionist movement. There were, then, two different visions for "mandate Palestine." At times, during the inter-war period, the tension between supporters of these two visions broke out in violence. Britain vacillated on what to do. After WW II, when Britain was exhausted, it announced that it would turn the situation over to the United Nations, which now carried the responsibilities of the earlier League of Nations.

The UN then set up a Special Committee On Palestine (UNSCOP) to study the situation and recommend a way forward. Canada's representative on this committee was Supreme Court Justice Ivan Rand, but Lester Pearson, then Undersecretary of State for External Affairs, played an important role too. This committee, which may have been influenced by the ancient Jewish ties with the land and the horror of the Holocaust, called for a partition of the land and the creation of two states: a state of Israel and an Arab state. The state of Israel was to get 56% of "mandate Palestine," though at this time Jewish people still represented less than one-third of the population. The Arab state would have the rest. The city of Jerusalem would not belong to either state; it would be an international zone.

Zionist leaders welcomed the plan as a step in the right direction, but Arab Palestinians and the governments of Arab countries opposed it. They saw it as an egregious colonial imposition. Nevertheless, in November 1947 the General Assembly of the United Nations approved this partition plan, in Resolution 181, thanks to exceptional lobbying by the USA. In mid-May 1948, when Britain formally withdrew, Zionist groups in Palestine declared the creation of the state of Israel and, according to Israeli historian Ilan Pappé, began to force out many of the Arab people living in what would

Palestine and Israel

now be the territory of the new state of Israel. Arab governments in the region began to fight back, but Jewish groups were armed and prepared, and when an armistice was agreed on in January 1949, Israel had increased its territory to 77% of mandate Palestine, and over 725,000 Palestinian Arabs had become refugees. It was their situation that led MCC, in that same year, to begin providing relief, education, health care, and agricultural development. MCC started this work in the West Bank and Jordan. Years later, MCC would also work in other parts of the Middle East.

In the years after the armistice, there was talk among Palestinian refugees and Arab governments about liberating Palestine, meaning the destruction of Israel as a Jewish state. The threats were evident in the rhetoric as well as in actions. In this context, in June 1967 Israel took the initiative. After six days of intense fighting it had won major military victories and gained control of all of Jerusalem, the West Bank,* Gaza, and other territories. In the following weeks and months there were extensive diplomatic discussions. Finally, in November 1967, the UN Security Council passed resolution 242. It called on Israel to withdraw from the territories that it had occupied in the 1967 war and, by implication, it also called on the world, including the Arab countries, to accept Israel, meaning Israel within the borders it had had before that war.

These two principles represent the oft-mentioned "land for peace" idea. This idea had implications for both Israel and the Palestinians. For Israel, it meant giving up the land that it had conquered in 1967, but on the remaining land, which was still 77% of mandate Palestine, it was to be able to live securely and in peace. For the Palestinians, it meant giving up their claim to land held by Israel before 1967 and in return they were to be able to live freely on the remaining 23% of mandate Palestine. Resolution 242 also called for a just resolution of the Palestinian refugee problem. These points, plus Resolution 338, which was passed after the 1973

---

* The West Bank refers to the area west of the Jordan River reaching until the pre-1967 border of Israel. As noted it was 23% of "mandate Palestine."

war and called for negotiations, became key elements in many of the later 'peace plans'. They pointed to the 'two-state solution' idea.

Essentially, these UN resolutions and the two-state idea were the basis of Canada's policy during all my years in the MCC office. In our advocacy work we tended not to challenge these principles; rather, our appeals were that they, and other principles of international law, be followed and upheld. This is not to say that we were committed to the two-state idea in an absolute sense; our commitment was to the well-being of people and their basic rights, but by accepting these ideas, we accepted the state of Israel within the 1967 borders and opposed its expansion beyond those borders.

Governmental Interest in our Stories: the 1970s and '80s

As we did with MCC workers from other areas of the world, when they returned we arranged meetings for them so that they could talk to officials and MPs about what they had seen and heard. In the case of the Middle East, we did that also for some Palestinians associated with MCC in the field. This, together with the close relations that some Canadian MCC workers in the field had with Canadian Embassy officials, meant that officials in Ottawa knew about MCC and our views.

This led to a particular development in 1979. In the election that year, Joe Clark, leader of the Progressive Conservative party promised to move the Canadian Embassy in Israel from Tel Aviv to Jerusalem. When he won that election, albeit with a minority government, prominent people began to ask that he reconsider that promise. We in MCC prepared a letter which was sent over the name of J. M. Klassen, our Executive Director. When the controversy heated up, Mr. Clark finally asked his predecessor, Robert Stanfield, to conduct a study of the issue. Michael Bell, a young Foreign Service Officer whom we had met recently, was assigned to assist Mr. Stanfield. Bell then invited us to meet with Mr. Stanfield.

This was a significant opportunity. We invited MCC's strongest voices to Ottawa for this meeting, notably, Frank H. Epp a member of the MCCC board who had written several books on the conflict;

Urbane Peachy, who had long served as MCC's director in the region; and J. M. Klassen. Our primary argument was that to move the Embassy to Jerusalem would be seen as endorsing Israel's claim over the city, thus violating UN Resolution 242, and as profoundly disrespectful of the rights of the Palestinian people and the views of the larger Arab world. As such, we said, the move would be a huge blow to the prospects for an agreement acceptable to both sides. In the end Mr. Stanfield's study recommended that the Embassy remain in Tel Aviv. Our meeting with him was only one factor contributing to that policy reversal, but at the time MCC was one of very few Canadian organizations working with the Palestinian people. Michael Bell, who later served as Canada's Ambassador in Israel, Jordan, and Egypt, became a life-long friend to a number of MCCers. He died in 2017 at the age of 73.

In the 1980s, there was a remarkable parallel between our work with officials in Ottawa and the relationships on the field between Canadian MCCers and Canadian Embassy officials. These MCC workers, such as Harold and Judy Dueck and Kathy Bergen, provided Embassy officials with a better window on the Palestinians. Some years later when I commended one official, Michel de Salaberry, on CIDA's program, he said, "when we planned our program to assist the Palestinian people we modelled it on yours." We were also able to do some work with Members of Parliament. Several times when we heard that a Parliamentary delegation was planning to visit the region, we were able to arrange for them to have a tour, led by MCCers in the field, to show them MCC's work with the Palestinians and to give them a window on Palestinian realities. Invariably, they described their time with the MCCers as a highlight.

In those years, the people in government, both officials and Parliamentarians, seemed to have a genuine hope that a settlement roughly acceptable to both sides was possible. To that end they were open and interested in hearing us. And we, thanks to our extensive on-the-ground relationships with Palestinians and our work in Ottawa, were able to help nurture that hope and spell out the issues that needed attention.

Supporting Steps Toward a Resolution: Late 1980s and Early '90s

In the late 1980s, the prospects for a "two-state" solution seemed to gain strength. The Palestinian intifada, a largely non-violent mass resistance movement aimed at ending Israel's 1967 occupation of the West Bank, continued for three years and won considerable international sympathy. And Palestinian leaders, at their 1988 National Congress in Algiers, accepted Resolutions 242 and 338. This was a major step. For Palestinians, to accept the state of Israel on these terms meant saying good-bye to villages, orchards, and other places that had marked their home since time immemorial.

Israel and various western governments professed skepticism about these Palestinian moves. Were the Palestinians really willing to accept Israel? Joe Clark, now Canada's External Affairs Minister, wanted to extend a modest acknowledgement toward the Palestinians and the steps they had taken. It could build trust. With this in mind, he decided to meet with a prominent Palestinian leader who was not a member of the Palestinian Liberation Organization. Faisal Husseini was such a person. Their meeting had to be at a neutral site. At the suggestion of Michel de Salaberry, they agreed on the MCC offices in East Jerusalem. The meeting took place in November 1990.

Ironically, the Gulf War in early 1991 also strengthened the prospects for a Palestinian-Israeli peace agreement. The stated American objective in that war was to push Iraq out of Kuwait. In the months leading up to the war the US managed to gain the support of most Arab countries. But in doing so the Americans and their supporters had to acknowledge a glaring double standard: if Iraq's occupation of Kuwait was unacceptable, then Israel's occupation of the West Bank and Gaza was unacceptable too. This led to a major international conference in Madrid, Spain in late 1991, co-sponsored by the US and the Soviet Union. Palestinian leaders felt that here, as never before, they were able to tell their side of the story to the international community. Here too, a process involving the international community was set up to work on different issues.

Palestine and Israel 69

This "peace process" led to a certain optimism.

The Canadian government wanted to contribute. Two initiatives at this time led to discussions with us in MCC. One came from CIDA's bilateral division. Officials there suggested that Canadian NGOs form a coalition which they would fund to do development and peace-building work in the Occupied Territories and to help fly the flag of Canada's new commitment. This was similar to what CIDA had done in Cambodia, but here the situation was different. There were many more Palestinian organizations in the West Bank and Gaza, as well as a number of Palestinian groups in Canada. And many of these had sharp political affiliations. MCC in the field had long been very careful about the kind of local organizations it would support; they had to be compatible with MCC's values and approach. The proposed Canada-based coalition would not carry the same concerns. We worked hard to satisfy the concerns of MCC on the field while still trying to help the Canadian government to increase its involvement. In the end, this coalition did not materialize, in part because of the formation of the Palestinian Authority (PA) after the 1993 Oslo Accords. Since the PA was somewhat like a government, Canada would work with it directly.

The other initiative related to the multilateral Working Group on Refugees. It was one of several working groups set up to address particular issues that came out of the Madrid Conference and the Oslo Accords. This working group, chaired by Canada, was to find a way of addressing the problem of Palestinian refugees whose numbers had grown to several million from the 725,000 in 1949. Most lived in the West Bank, Jordan, and Lebanon, but many were scattered elsewhere. Resolution 194, adopted by the UN General Assembly in 1948, stated that they had a "right of return," but it was clear that Israel and its supporters would resist their actual return.

This led to the view that the refugees' right of return should be acknowledged but in practice the people should be given options, such as resettlement abroad. The hope was that if they were offered generous assistance to get resettled elsewhere, they would chose not to return to what was now the state of Israel. Canadian officials then inquired whether MCC, with its high credibility in the region and its experience in resettling refugees in Canada, would help in implementing this plan if it were formally approved. Alas, other problems arose and the plan never got to the point where MCC had to give a clear response to this idea.

In the second half of the 1990s, the prospects for the two-state solution faded. Israel had withdrawn from some areas, but in the West Bank it continued to build more settlements and by-pass roads, to impose closures, curfews and check points on Palestinian roads, and to divert the water resources—so much so that the Palestinians did not always have enough to do household laundry. Social, educational, and economic life for the Palestinian people became increasingly difficult. In Gaza, a strip 41 km long and 6–12 km wide, which in 2018 was home to nearly two million Palestinians, restrictions were even more severe. Some began to refer to Gaza as a prison.

Of course Palestinians resisted where they could; some used violence, causing injury and death among Israelis. We certainly did not condone that, but we felt that in the overall situation Israel's expansion beyond the 1967 borders and its various restrictions on Palestinian life represented the more basic problem. Accordingly, our main message to Canadian authorities was to ask that they press the Israeli government. We did this with letters, with meetings for returning workers, and by working with other organizations.

One particular development, in the fall of 1996, involved a proposal for a Canada-Israel Free Trade Agreement (CIFTA). In effect CIFTA deemed goods produced in Israeli settlements in the Occupied Territories to be Israeli goods, thereby conferring a legitimacy on those settlements in violation of international law and established Canadian policy. I returned from a trip to the region just as CIFTA was being considered, so I appeared before committees of both the House of Commons and the Senate, but it was approved anyway.

Challenging the New Restrictions, After the Mid-1990s

Western governments in their official statements, continued to favour the two-state solution, but Israel, instead of moving to end the occupation, deepened its hold on the territories. It seemed important to speak against this renewed repression. I was helped by the fact that my family and I had lived in the region for two years in the early-1990s. Thus, I devoted quite a lot of time to the Palestine-Israel issue, working not only in MCC but in several NGO coalitions.

In late September of 2000, a second Palestinian intifada began. It appeared less committed to nonviolence than the first. Not surprisingly, the Israelis responded strongly. The 30-member delegate body of MCCC held its annual meeting in November, so I drafted a substantial letter addressed to Prime Minister Chrétien. The letter referred to MCC's now 50-year involvement with the Palestinian people, described the recent developments, and identified specific elements necessary for peace. It stated in part:

> ... [T]he violence that broke out in late September has troubled us deeply. By now nearly 300 people have been killed and over 10,000 injured. Much property has been destroyed ... a peace that is just for both the Palestinians and the Israelis ... would be advanced by a full Israeli withdrawal from the Palestinian territories over which it gained control in the 1967 war.... We would urge you, then, to call strongly for an end to the 1967 occupation. This would be in keeping with the UN Resolution 242, passed in 1967 which the Canadian government has always supported.... In addition ... there must be a fair settlement for the Palestinian refugees who now number over four million... There must also be a shared arrangement for Jerusalem, one that respects both peoples and all three faiths and ensures that the city is accessible to all ...

One coalition I was active in during these years was The NGO Middle East Working Group. In the spring of 2001, we prepared a brief of about 3,500 words entitled "A Call for Canadian Initiatives on the Middle East." We had 18 recommendations. Significantly, External Affairs officials agreed to meet with us in a day-long session to discuss them. The meeting, on April 23, 2001, was co-chaired by Mike Molloy, Canada's Special Envoy to the Middle East Peace Process, and me. It included about 15 NGO representatives and about ten government officials. One memorable part was a debate, not between us and the officials but among the officials, about the merits of our recommendations. Molloy expressed himself forcefully to his colleagues, saying that he'd much rather work on the basis of our recommendations than from the existing policy of the government.

I was also active in the Canadian ecumenical coalition "Kairos" and in its subcommittee on the Middle East. There, in early 2002, we, particularly Dale Hildebrandt and I, drafted a policy statement called "Our Continuing Hope for a Just Peace in the Palestinian/Israeli Conflict". It began with two quotations from the Bible: "Comfort, comfort my people, says your God. Speak tenderly to Jerusalem and cry that her warfare is ended…" (Isaiah 40:2); and the words of Jesus, "O Jerusalem, Jerusalem,… how often would I have gathered your children together as a hen gathers her brood under her wings …" (Matthew 23:37). The paper then outlined various aspects of a Biblical vision for peace and how they might apply to the current Israeli/Palestinian conflict. The Kairos board approved it on September 17, 2002.

Tragically, at this time many aspects of international relations became more militarized. This happened because, in response to the horrific attacks on the World Trade Center in New York on September 11, 2001, the US made "war on terrorism" its dominant foreign policy theme. Leaders in a number of countries bought into this rhetoric; they could now glibly label opponents as terrorists and thus align themselves with the US. This helped some Israeli leaders to dismiss Palestinian resistance, even if a Palestinian farmer was merely trying to prevent some ancestral land from being taken for a new Israeli settlement.

Palestine and Israel

By 2002 and 2003, Israel was actively building "the Wall," also called "the separation barrier." In densely populated areas it was made of concrete and measured eight metres high. At other places it was electrified barbed wire. Instead of strictly following the 1967 boundary, at places the Wall wound its way deep into the West Bank, thus depriving the Palestinians of even more land and water resources. We then, among other things, joined leaders of eight Canadian NGOs in a November 3, 2003 letter to the new Foreign Affairs Minister, Bill Graham, asking him to press Israel to cease construction of the Wall. The letter described it as "illegal under international law." The letter also referred to Israel's escalating use of "targeted assassinations" and its "increasing willingness to inflict death and injury on Palestinian civilians … and the massive and systematic destruction of Palestinian homes."

Later that year, when Hamas won the Palestinian legislative elections, Canada immediately suspended its aid. Other western countries followed. They wanted Hamas to renounce violence and to recognize Israel. We had no quarrel with these objectives, but in our letters we argued that Canada and other western countries should also press Israel to end its harsh occupation, pull back to its pre-1967 borders, and recognize the right of the Palestinians to have a state on the rest.

In the following year the Palestinians formed a new government. We felt it met the stated conditions, so we supported an ecumenical letter to Prime Minister Harper urging Canada to resume its aid program, to call on all elements in the Palestinian Authority to recognize the state of Israel on its pre-1967 borders, and to urge all parties to begin peace negotiations on the basis of Resolution 242 and other principles of international law.

Sadly, no such progress toward peace could be seen. Israel continued to extend its hold on the territories, leaving the Palestinians with little more than half of what would have been their state according to Resolution 242, and with many restrictions even inside that limited space. Their situation was articulated in a moving way in 2009 by 13 heads of churches in Jerusalem in a widely circulated statement called "Kairos Palestine." Many longtime advocates now abandoned the two-state idea and looked for alternative formulations that might protect the basic rights of the people. Unfortunately, the alternatives faced serious obstacles too.

◆

In considering these profoundly tragic issues, western Christians should also acknowledge two background realities. One is the role of Christianity in the long history of anti-Semitism which, late in the 1800s, led Jewish leaders in Europe to begin pressing for the creation of the state of Israel. The other reality is contemporary Christian Zionism, some of which provides unqualified political support for the policies of the state of Israel and shows little regard for Arab people, be they Christian or Muslim. In my opinion, both of these issues reflect serious misinterpretations of the Bible and the message of Jesus, but a discussion of them lies outside the scope of this collection of stories.

7

IRAQ

◆

Our work in relation to Iraq began much later—only after it invaded Kuwait on August 2, 1990. The international community's response to this invasion was quick. Later that same day the UN Security Council passed a resolution calling on Iraq to withdraw and on both parties to work on their differences through negotiation. Just four days later, on August 6, under pressure from the US and Britain, the Security Council passed another resolution. This one imposed far-reaching sanctions on Iraq and threatened military action against Iraq if it did not withdraw. Canada was a strong supporter of the UN and a friend of the US so, if there would be military action, Canada might well participate. Many Canadians became worried. Various groups, including some MPs and a Christian Peacemaker Teams delegation, travelled to Iraq in the hope of preventing war.

The 1990-91 Invasions
The board of MCCC was scheduled to meet on September 6. We prepared a two-page letter to the Prime Minister which the board then approved. The letter acknowledged that Iraq's invasion of Kuwait was wrong and that Saddam Hussein was an oppressive dictator but held that our long involvement in the region gave us many reasons to question the wisdom of military action. We

endorsed "certain economic sanctions" but suggested that the industrialized world's selfish interest in oil was behind the apparent move towards military action. Such action, we argued, would "strengthen new extremists ... and result in widespread resentment against the West." We called for attention to historic and underlying grievances and for "greater reliance on negotiation, even if it takes time." One reason why Iraq had invaded Kuwait is that Kuwait had taken steps relating to oil that hurt Iraq economically. At this time Iraq desperately needed all possible revenues, because for most of the 1980s it had been engaged in a very costly war with Iran. (Some estimates claim that one million people died in that war.)

During the fall of 1990, when the momentum toward war against Iraq continued building we sent a second letter to the Canadian government. Dated October 31, it stated again that "Iraq's actions against Kuwait are wrong" but pleaded that the world not respond by going to war. "The consequences of war would be catastrophic," we argued, making many of the problems in the region "much more intractable!" We also argued that while "the borders of Kuwait, like those of any other state, should be respected, this is not the highest good." We referred to the need for the West to do more to achieve a just settlement on the Palestinian-Israeli conflict and to recognize historic issues in the Gulf region. On January 11, 1991, when war seemed imminent, we sent a third letter, arguing again that diplomatic efforts and economic sanctions had not been exhausted.

On January 17, the US-led coalition, having assembled a massive array of military equipment in the region, began its attack. It had the legal umbrella of UN Security Council resolutions and the active support of more than 30 countries including Canada. Most Arab governments were supportive too. Since the MCCC board was holding its annual meeting on January 18 and 19, we prepared a three-page statement directed primarily at constituent churches to explain what we in MCCC had done, why we believed that this military action would lead to more problems, that we anticipated huge relief needs once the fighting stopped, that it was important to try to build bridges with people from the Middle East living in

Canada, and that the historic stance of our churches regarding war continued to be important.

In late February, the fighting on the part of the coalition ended; Iraq was pushed out of Kuwait. But the death toll, if the uprisings in the weeks that followed are included, was believed to be over 100,000. We then wrote to the government and called for a substantial three-pronged response: to alleviate the immediate humanitarian needs; to ensure longer term economic and social rehabilitation; and to work with other countries for disarmament throughout the Middle East. MCC also invited several Middle East people to visit churches in North America to talk about how the war was seen there. We arranged for these visitors to come to Ottawa and meet with government personnel. We also arranged meetings in Ottawa for Carol McLean, an MCC public health nurse, who spent six weeks in Iraq surveying the needs, and for Ed Epp, MCC director in Jordan, who had witnessed the massive influx of Iraqis into Jordan and who, in visiting Iraq, had seen the desperate situation of the Kurdish and Shia people who had hoped that this war would liberate them of Saddam Hussein's oppressive rule.

To advocate for a generous post-war response was easy, but the earlier advocacy against this war was challenging. A number of people with whom we had long felt a like-mindedness believed that the war was justified. Often their reasoning related to the prospects for a new international order. With the end of the Cold War that had long polarized international relations, it was believed that the United Nations would now, finally, be able to fulfill its original purposes of resolving conflicts, securing peace, and strengthening international law and human rights. Saddam Hussein stood in grave violation of these principles. He was a brutal and oppressive ruler, and his invasion of another country was a serious matter. Was it not necessary to get him to withdraw, and did his apparent unwillingness to do that not justify military force? If we supported the idea of a "rules-based international system," did that not mean that sometimes basic rules had to be enforced? And this initiative, though led by the US, had broad international support and was approved by the UN Security Council. How could we be against it?

We did not have answers to all of these questions, although we felt there were more elements that needed consideration. Could some of the reasons why Saddam Hussein had invaded Kuwait not be addressed? And did his offer, made on the eve of the war, to withdraw from Kuwait if Israel would withdraw from the territories that it occupied in the 1967 war, not merit discussion? Certainly, this made him popular with the Palestinians and with many other Arab people. Israel would have none of that, and leaders of the international coalition quickly rejected the offer with the argument that to accept it would reward Saddam Hussein for invading Kuwait. We did not have a formula for peace, but given MCC's long involvement in the region and our experience in various other parts of the world, we felt that a military invasion would create more problems than it would solve.

At the time of the military build-up, I also served on the Social Action Commission of the Evangelical Fellowship of Canada (EFC). In that role I drafted a letter which its leaders then sent to the Prime Minister. The letter acknowledged that some denominations of the EFC were committed to pacifism while others subscribed to the historic "just war" doctrine. Then it raised questions about whether a war in this situation could be justified on the basis of just war criteria, specifically: had all other options been exhausted? Did the build-up not suggest a vastly disproportionate use of force? Would there not be a large number of innocent people killed, etc.? The EFC letter also held that an invasion by western powers would probably make the historic Christian communities in the Middle East even more vulnerable.

A Decade of Sanctions

The fighting ended in late February 1991 but now the international coalition, under pressure from the US, got UN approval to tighten the sanctions further, not loosen them; also, the sanctions were given a new purpose. Now they were to pressure Iraq to allow UN inspectors to search the country for weapons of mass destruction

Iraq

which it was suspected of having. To administer the inspection program the UN set up a special commission called UNSCOM. Canada, being on the Security Council at this time, was represented on UNSCOM. Understandably, Iraqi authorities were wary of these probing inspections but by most accounts the inspectors eventually reached most of their stated goals. However, the US and some other countries felt that the sanctions should remain in place, lest Iraq try to develop such weapons in the future or rebuild itself as a major power in the region.

The continuing sanctions had a devastating effect on life in Iraq. It had been a modern society, with social and economic indicators close to those of some European countries. But now, unable to export oil, it could not rebuild the infrastructure that had been destroyed during the war; also, it was severely restricted in what it could import, even basic things like equipment for water purification, fertilizers, and other inputs for agriculture. Salaries for teachers, health workers, and civil servants were cut to a small fraction of what they had been. At one time Iraq had been a generous donor to the UN's World Food Program; now it was a needy recipient. It was a situation of 'de-development.' According to a 1995 UN report, one million Iraqis had died because of the sanctions. This led the UN in 1996 to create what was called the Oil for Food (OFF) program. It would allow Iraq to sell a limited amount of oil and then import more humanitarian goods, if those goods were approved by the UN Sanctions Committee in New York. In January of 1999, when Canada again gained a two-year seat on the UN Security Council, External Affairs Minister Lloyd Axworthy pressed hard for a review of the Iraq situation. This led to further modifications in the sanctions regime, but serious problems remained.

By 1999, MCC had almost a decade of experience with relief work in Iraq. During this time it had cooperated extensively with the Middle East Council of Churches (MECC). The reports from our own workers, from MECC staff, and from other sources, as well as my travels there in 1994 and 1999, enabled me to discuss the issues with External Affairs officials, MPs, and other NGOs. After my 1999 trip, I prepared a substantial letter to Mr. Axworthy. Dated November 29, it stated in part:

> A recent UNICEF survey found that the mortality rate for children under five has more than doubled in the last decade... School attendance, which was very high in the 1980's, has fallen substantially as children look for ways of gaining a livelihood. Stealing, prostitution and killing has increased. Two and one half million animals, 18% of the country's total, suffer from foot and mouth disease. Half of the palm trees have died. (These used to produce 80% of the world's dates.) Electricity production is at 40% of the earlier level. Unemployment is at least 65%.

Regarding the OFF program, we said that since it was "focussed on relief [it] provides very little for maintenance, rehabilitation or development. This has serious implications for the infrastructure relating to water purification, sanitation, irrigation, electricity, telecommunications, and education and health facilities, all of which need both normal maintenance and extensive repair from war damages." I also argued that the Sanctions Committee was too suspicious of the "dual use" potential of various items; for example, items meant for water purification systems would be barred with the claim that they could be used for chemical weapons. Our letter recommended an end to non-military sanctions.

A few months later, in March 2000, the Parliamentary Committee on Foreign Affairs held hearings on the Iraq situation. We had pushed for this. Now I worked with Dale Hildebrand of the ecumenical coalition, Inter-Church Action (ICA), in preparing a substantial brief. Dale and I presented it on March 21. We described the humanitarian devastation, quoting a recent report from the International Committee of the Red Cross that, "after nine years of trade sanctions ... the situation of the civilian population is increasingly desperate ... food shortages and the lack of medicines and clean drinking water threaten their very survival." We also quoted UN officials about the significant success of the weapons inspection program. One US inspector, Scott Ritter, who, from 1991 to 1998, was known as the toughest of inspectors, had stated in 1999 that Iraq had no meaningful weapons of mass destruction, whether biological, chemical, or nuclear, and that it had no capacity to produce them on a meaningful scale. We again called for an end to sanctions that affected the country's civilian life. The Parliamentary Committee heard us and made positive recommendations. Unfortunately, the government did not accept them.

There was another development. In 1998, the US claimed that Iraq was not cooperating adequately with the UN inspectors, most of whom were Americans. The UN Secretary General, Kofi Annan, did not see it that way at all; he appealed to the US for negotiations on the points of difference but the US insisted that all inspectors withdraw; then it and the UK began a bombing campaign they called "Desert Fox," echoing "Desert Storm," the name used for the 1991 invasion. The new bombing was said to be aimed at military installations, but at times it hit residential areas including hospitals and schools. The bombing was sporadic, not continuous, but the fly-overs were almost daily, creating widespread fear. Also around this time, US President Clinton stated that the sanctions would remain as long as Saddam Hussein remained in power. In 1998 he also signed the Iraq Liberation Act and allocated $98 million for training Iraqi exiles. These actions made a peaceful resolution much more difficult.

We continued to appeal to people in the Canadian government; we arranged meetings for a visiting Iraqi bishop and an aid worker from the Middle East Council of Churches; we worked closely with the ICA, as well as with other NGOs and Canadian Arab organizations. We did not want to defend the Iraqi government. In our ICA brief to the Parliamentary Committee we acknowledged "the Iraqi government's record of suppression and brutality." We said: "The massive killing of the Kurds, the forced relocation of tens of thousands of minority people and the torture and murder of dissenters, must not be minimized." But we argued that the existing sanctions regime did not address these concerns about the Iraqi government.

We were not alone in our view. In 1997, as part of an effort to improve things for ordinary people, the UN appointed Dennis Halliday to lead what was called the UN Humanitarian Program in Iraq. Halliday, from Ireland, had served with the UN for 30 years at senior levels. After one year in this position on Iraq, he resigned, stating that the sanctions were "genocidal." He added: "my innate sense of justice ... is outraged by the violence that the UN sanctions have brought ... upon the lives of children, families ... Some will tell you that the leadership is punishing the Iraqi people. That is not my perception...." The next person appointed to that UN position was Hans von Sponeck, from Germany, another veteran UN official. He resigned after 15 months for similar reasons. During his time in that position he visited Ottawa, met with Canadian government representatives, and boosted our own advocacy work.

People in the Canadian government were remarkably open to us during these years, both officials in the External Affairs department and advisers in the office of the External Affairs Minister, Lloyd Axworthy. (One advisor in his office was Dr. Eric Hoskins who, years later, would serve as Ontario's Minister of Health.) Axworthy certainly used the opportunity of Canada's two-year seat on the UN Security Council (1999 – 2000) to press for modifications in the Iraq sanctions system so as to ease their effect on civilians despite objections from the US. But in fairness, it was not only the US. Some Arab governments were also determined not to allow Saddam Hussein to become a strong regional player again. Israel was particularly concerned about that.

One conversation with Canada's representative on UNSCOM remains with me. He did not defend the way the regime of sanctions and inspections was being applied in Iraq, but he believed in the principle of a UN-based inspection system, charged with the task of certifying that a given country was free of weapons of mass destruction. He said, "if that can done for one country, then it can be done for others; eventually, this could help us to clear the world of weapons of mass destruction." It is an appealing idea but it would have more credibility if the countries insisting on the sanctions took serious steps to dispose of their own weapons of mass destruction.

The 2003 Invasion

Soon after the attacks on the World Trade Towers in New York on September 11, 2001, the "war on terror" became a primary principle of US foreign policy. By October 7, the US led an invasion of Afghanistan because the Taliban government there had connections with Osama bin Laden, reputedly the leader of those responsible for the attacks.

We prepared a two-page letter addressed to Prime Minister Jean Chrétien about the war on terror approach, for consideration by the MCCC delegate body at its annual meeting on November 24, 2001. The delegate body approved the letter. It referred to our theological teachings:

> that all people bear the image of God, that we are to love our neighbours as ourselves, that the standards by which we judge the actions of others must also apply to us, that the resources of the world are for the well-being of all people, and that God continues to work in human affairs, even in difficult situations, inviting people to seek peace, justice and reconciliation.

From this perspective we argued, "There seems to be far too much faith in the efficacy of military action.... The focus is too much on only some acts of terrorism.... The injustice of the international economic system should be recognized as one reason for the anger against the West.... The war may cause a deterioration in inter-religious relations."

Soon there were signs that the US was preparing to attack Iraq as well, claiming that it was involved in the 9/11 attacks and building weapons of mass destruction and promoting terrorism. This time, it did not get UN authorization but, together with Britain, gathered a "coalition of the willing." Whether Canada would join was an open question. On March 12, 2002 we sent a three-page letter, signed by the MCCC Executive Director, Don Peters, to the Prime Minister and the Minister for Foreign Affairs. The letter stated: "We are deeply concerned about the prospect of a US-led military action against Iraq aimed at bringing about a 'regime change'. We commend you for opposing this course of action and urge you to make every effort to dissuade the American government from pursuing it." After outlining our reasons, we concluded, "Wars often take unanticipated turns, solve fewer problems than expected, and unleash unforeseen negative dynamics with far-reaching consequences."

As the move toward war continued, we were involved with several other organizations in preparing letters, including the CCIC, the North-South Institute, and Project Ploughshares, where I still served on the board. A three-page January 8, 2003 letter to the Prime Minister, signed also by representatives of Kairos, World Vision, a Canadian Arab organization, MCC, and several others, stated in part:

> Though the present moment is marked by the prospect of a terrible war, it is also marked by an unusual engagement on the part of both the international community and the Arab world. This, we submit, reduces the grounds for war and holds the potential for pursuing alternatives more effectively, not only for Iraq and the Palestinian/Israeli situations but, more broadly, for the promotion of justice, human rights, regional disarmament, adherence to law, responsible government, and economic development.... Canada must help the world to turn away from an orientation that seeks security primarily in the power to repress and intimidate... Canada must resist the view that people from different cultures and civilizations are doomed to endless suspicion and hostility. It must give expression to its faith that this world is a place for all

people.

On January 31, 2003 we sent a two-page letter signed by the leaders of the eight largest Mennonite and Brethren in Christ groups in Canada as well as by MCCC leaders. It stated in part:

> We do not dismiss the claim that the Iraqi people have long suffered under a very oppressive government, even though some criticisms against it appear selective and self-serving. Nor do we propose quick and certain alternative method for achieving the desired changes. Nevertheless, we believe that a war would make things much worse.... Instead of reducing the threat of terrorism, a war on Iraq could increase it. In our view the 'war on terrorism' begun in the fall of 2001, has relied too much on military might and too little on addressing 'root causes'. This approach has deepened hostility toward the West and encouraged the West to see the rest of the world as a source of threats, thereby deepening an ominous divide. Already we see increased vulnerability to minorities....

At one point during these months, a Canadian Arab organization, which had invited a delegation of Iraqi church leaders to Ottawa, asked me to arrange a luncheon where they could meet with local church leaders. The Iraqi church leaders spoke of the two decades of suffering of their people, starting in the early 1980s with the Iran-Iraq war and continuing through the 1991 Gulf War and the 1990s decade of sanctions. The Bishop of the Chaldean church said very simply, "Anyone can start a war but no one can say how it will end." He died just a few weeks later. Another person in that meeting, Rev. Youssef Adel from the Assyrian Orthodox church, was murdered amid the violence in Bagdad in 2008.

On March 20, 2003, when the US-led "coalition of the willing" invaded Iraq, Canada did not participate. The government had wavered, but at the last minute, Prime Minister Chrétien decided against joining. Sometime later he commented that he had been influenced by the voice of Canada's faith community. However,

Canada wanted to remain on good terms with the US. So when the military coalition announced its victory, Canada committed itself to providing substantial assistance towards the rehabilitation of the country. I was then invited to several meetings hosted by External Affairs and CIDA officials to discuss the form that such assistance might take. I also made a point of having MCC workers who had returned from Iraq come to Ottawa and speak with officials. Most CIDA officials were very interested in hearing their views on how Canada might be involved.

In September of that year, just five months after that invasion, I had the privilege of participating in an MCC delegation to Iraq. To my surprise, many of the Iraqis with whom we met were grateful to the Americans for overthrowing Saddam Hussein. Life under his dictatorial rule had been so harsh. But we also heard deep concern about "mistakes" that the new occupying administration was making, including the disbanding of security forces; the failure to prevent widespread looting of museums, universities, and hospitals; and the general "de-Baathification" policy, meaning that no one who had been a member of Saddam Hussein's Baath party would have a place in the new governmental structures. People in Iraq's military forces were also dismissed.

These policies were disastrous. They left several hundred thousand well-trained people unemployed, even though most had no particular loyalty to Saddam Hussein; many had joined the Baath party in order to get jobs. Now these people had to fend for themselves; before long there were various militia groups and weapons seemed readily available. For several years violence and destruction seemed to envelope the country. Hundreds of thousands were killed. Christians were certainly not the only ones affected but in some areas the historic Christian groups became targets. It is believed that over next decade at least three-quarters of the 1.5 million Christians who lived in Iraq before the war fled the country, never to return. Many Muslims left too. Vast numbers went to neighbouring countries, especially Jordan, or became internally displaced. In this context it was difficult to mount the

Iraq

needed reconstruction efforts.

It is ironic that while some senior American administrators adopted disastrous policies, other Americans genuinely believed they were liberating the country from the oppressive rule of Saddam Hussein and giving the people a chance for a better future. Some of the post-war initiatives were good. But in the overall context, few could be brought to full fruition. Would other ways of working towards a liberation of the Iraqi people have been possible? Certainly, the flow of weapons to Iraq and to the region generally should have been stopped decades earlier. Also needed is a sustained commitment by the international community to press for human rights and international law throughout the region; indeed, throughout the world.

8

NORTH KOREA

◆

The Canadian Foodgrains Bank (CFGB) had started shipping food aid to North Korea soon after that country's appeal in 1995. The CFGB partners most active in this effort were the United and Presbyterian churches and MCCC. But they could use only their own church funds for it. The government would not allow them to use any CIDA money in North Korea. Marvin Frey, the Executive Director of MCCC, then asked me to work on persuading the government to change that policy and allow CIDA money to be used there.

    A key reason why Canada held North Korea to be ineligible for government money was that it represented a threat to South Korea. South Korea was Canada's sixth-largest trading partner and Canada had a long-standing commitment to its security. For us, then, a key question was whether South Korea could be persuaded to send a "green light" to the Canadian government about the idea of changing its policy so as to allow NGOs to use CIDA money for humanitarian aid for the North. To pursue this question I arranged for CFGB representatives to meet with officials of the South Korean Embassy. We wanted to assure them that the CFGB did not have a political agenda and that our objective was only to follow the Christian calling of its member churches to feed the hungry. Interestingly, in our meeting at the Embassy, after we as CFGB representatives had introduced ourselves, the South Korean official made a point of telling us that he too was a Christian believer and that he and the South Korean people generally felt a lot of compassion for the people of the North, but they had to be careful about anything that could affect the security of South Korea.

There were other background factors. The Presbyterian and United churches had done a lot of missionary work in what was now North Korea in the generations before World War I. In recent decades, they and the World Council of Churches had worked hard to build connections with the few churches still there. Also interesting is that Canada's External Affairs minister at this time, the Hon. Lloyd Axworthy, was a member of the United Church and that a key official in Canada's External Affairs department was Bruce Jutzi, a former MCC worker. I continued to communicate with the official at the South Korean Embassy, and a few weeks after our meeting there, Bruce called me to say that they had received a note from the Embassy saying that they would not object if the Canadian government allowed its funds to be used for humanitarian relief in the North.

In the summer of 1997 I was invited to join a small CFGB delegation in a visit to North Korea. Seeing the effects of food shortages on children was particularly moving. Upon my return I spoke in a number of churches and wrote an Op-Ed piece for the *Globe and Mail* newspaper, trying to build popular support for the government's new policy regarding money for NGOs and for an increase in its allocations to the World Food Programme in North Korea. In several churches where I spoke, a number of immigrants from South Korea attended. They were sympathetic but had concerns about whether the government in the North might divert our aid to its army. There was no fully satisfactory answer to this question, but I would tell people that we had seen the CFGB bags of grain going to orphanages and village people; also, that since the North Korean government was committed to feeding its army first, it would use its own food resources for that purpose, meaning that the people would get only what was left. On that basis, I felt, the food aid we sent was likely to increase the amount available for the people without affecting the amount going to the army.

At this time, some Canadian churches and non-governmental groups became interested in developing people-to-people relations with North Korea. This led to the formation of the "Canada – DPR Korea Association." (North Korea's official name is the Democratic People's Republic of Korea. Hence, DPRK.) MCC's Asia desk encouraged me to participate, so I served on the board of this Association for a few years. In this capacity, I ended up hosting a reception for the North Korean Ambassador on his first visit to Canada. (He was the DPRK's Ambassador to the UN but was now also seeking accreditation to Canada.) We had the reception on a Sunday afternoon in June 2002 in the offices of the United Nations Association of Canada. Approximately 20 guests attended, including several from NGOs and Human Rights organizations, as well as retired diplomats like Geoffrey Pearson, whose longstanding interest in our work had made him a helpful counsellor.

The reception was the result of a 2001 decision by Minister Axworthy to establish diplomatic relations with the DPRK. This reflected the cautious hopefulness of the time. Maybe we were starting a new chapter. Unfortunately, it did not last. I do not know all the reasons. Did North Korea's leaders become uneasy about this increased exposure to foreigners?

9

The USSR

◆

In the decades before the collapse of the Soviet Union in 1991, it was seen as the primary threat to western countries including Canada. We in MCC spoke to that in our statements on Canada's foreign and defence policies. But the fact that there were thousands of Mennonites and people of Mennonite background still living in the Soviet Union gave rise to more particular concerns, as reflected in the three stories recounted here.

"The Christians Are Our Best Workers"
The situation of Christian believers in the Soviet Union fluctuated. At times they could gather and worship, albeit under various restrictions; at other times they were persecuted.

The late 1970s were a more difficult time. Ministers were imprisoned and congregations harassed. Early in 1980 MCC workers who followed those developments compiled a list of over thirty Mennonite ministers who had been imprisoned. MCC then requested that we in the Ottawa Office register a concern about this with the Soviet Embassy in Ottawa.

Thus, in March of that year, I called the Embassy and asked if we could meet with them. They agreed, so Freda Enns and I went over at the appointed time. We knew it would be delicate. After all, our message implied a criticism of their government. We wanted to ask the Embassy officials to ask officials in Moscow to look into the situation of these imprisoned ministers.

Two Embassy officials received us. I referred to the history of Mennonites in their country and explained our current concern as respectfully as I could. They asked some questions but it was a moderate exchange. Then the Ambassador, Alexander Yacovlev, walked into the room. He was a short, heavy-set man who walked with a cane; he had big bushy eyebrows, a strong voice, and a commanding personality. Having served in Ottawa longer than any other Ambassador, he was considered the dean of the diplomatic corps.

Yacovlev took a chair close to mine and spoke directly and emphatically, saying: "Do you personally know the people on your list?" Obviously I did not. "That means," he continued, "that you do not know everything about their situation. So you have to admit that there is at least a possibility that they are in prison for reasons other than church activities. Perhaps they were involved in hooliganism or other illegal activities."

I explained that I had a lot of confidence in my colleagues who had gathered this information, that our organization had a long and honourable record in many parts of the world; that we were not on a crusade; that we were not going public and trying to embarrass their government; and that we would not submit this list unless we were very sure that our information was well founded. After some back and forth, he agreed to ask his colleagues in Moscow to check into things.

Then he came to his main point, which I remember as follows:

> You Christians in the West, you do not understand the attitude of my government towards the Christians in my country. You think my government hates the Christians. That is not true at all! My government likes the Christians. They are our best workers. They do not come to work drunk. They arrive on time. They do not steal from the factories. They are reliable. They are not always

quarrelling and fighting. They are our best workers. My government likes them a great deal. Our economy would be in big trouble if it was not for our Christian workers. It is time that you Christians in the West understood that!

Having made his point, the Ambassador left the room and the meeting soon ended. Aside from feeling humiliated for having been spoken to so forcefully, I was deeply moved by the witness of the Christians in the Soviet Union reflected in the Ambassador's words. Even though they lived with many restrictions, including closed doors to higher education and the professions, the witness of their integrity in daily life was noticed by Soviet authorities at the highest levels.

In 1983, Ambassador Yacovlev was called back to Moscow. Some years after that I read reports that he was the architect of the more open policies that President Gorbachev adopted in the later 1980s. There were reports, too, that while in Canada he had been personal friends with the family of Prime Minister Trudeau and his Agriculture Minister, Eugene Whelan.

When he died in October 2005, the Guardian newspaper reported that he had "turned fiercely not only against Bolshevism but Marxism itself ..." and had "championed the idea that universal values should take precedence over class struggle." As a youth he had been an exchange student in the US.

A Different Form of Advocacy
Some Christian groups in the West took a different approach toward religious freedom in the Soviet Union. Early in 1976, two men connected to a southern Ontario Mennonite Brethren church approached us about helping to organize an effort to press for the release of Georgi Vins, who was in a Soviet prison.

Vins was of Mennonite Brethren background. His father and grandfather, Peter and Jacob Wiens, respectively, had come to Canada in the 1920s but both had returned to the Soviet Union to do evangelistic work. One of them died in a Siberian prison in 1943.

Years later, Georgi Vins had become the leader of an unregistered Baptist group.

His imprisonment had received considerable publicity. *Time* magazine carried a story about him, and the World Council of Churches had appealed to Soviet authorities on his behalf. But his strongest advocates were people connected with an organization called Underground Evangelism (UE). Among other things, they now planned to hold rallies in front of Soviet Embassies in 13 countries on the same day to press for Vins's release.

How was I to respond to these two men from southern Ontario? My superiors in MCC, though sympathetic to Vins's situation, were not keen on the methods of UE. We decided that we would arrange a meeting for them with External Affairs officials, but with regard to the Soviet Embassy we would write our own letter to the Ambassador. When we then met with External Affairs officials, they reported that they were in regular discussion with Soviet authorities in which they pressed for human rights, religious freedom, emigration permits, family reunification, and other issues. They also reported progress on various individual cases and explained that if they made a really big fuss about Georgi Vins and publicly embarrassed the Soviets, then, even if successful, they might have more difficulty working with them on other cases.

Around this time, this UE group's plans for a big rally in Ottawa hit a snag. Officials from the Department of Revenue visited its offices and advised them that if they went ahead with the rally, their charitable tax status might be in jeopardy. This caused a small storm of its own. Could charitable organizations never organize rallies? Questions were asked in the House of Commons. The *Globe and Mail*, had an editorial about it, on May 14, 1976. We in MCC also wrote to the government.

Some weeks later, the UE Ottawa rally did take place, but in a very low-key way. As for Georgi Vins, a few years later, near the end of Jimmy Carter's presidency, the Soviets agreed to exchange him and several other dissidents for two of their spies held in a US prison. Vins then settled in Elkhart, Indiana, where he associated with a Baptist church and led an organization called Russian Gospel Ministries. He died in 1998. Reportedly, some of his papers are in the Mennonite Brethren Archives in Winnipeg.

And what about the two men who first approached us back in 1976? One was Helmuth Buxbaum, who had become wealthy from a chain of nursing homes he owned. The other man was Rudy Janzen, a Mennonite Brethren minister. I felt Rudy wanted to "walk with" Buxbaum, a newcomer to their church, while also helping him to see the Vins situation in the larger Mennonite context. Buxbaum may have been impatient with that. Soon after our encounter, he left the Mennonite Brethren church and joined a Baptist group. Also, he may have had other struggles. In 1986, he was convicted for arranging the killing of his wife. He died in prison in 2007.

The story leaves one with a distinct sadness, especially for Buxbaum's wife, but also for Buxbaum himself and for those who tried to walk with him. The question of how to support the human rights of Christians and others in totalitarian countries remains.

Other Interactions in Relation to the Soviet Union
Given that many Mennonites in Canada had come from the Soviet Union after each of the two world wars, there was ongoing interest in relating to and supporting the Mennonites still there. Fortunately, despite being quite closed, it was possible for Mennonite leaders from Canada to make occasional visits there and also for their church leaders to visit Canada.

When church leaders from the Soviet Union visited Canada, they would spend most of their time in Mennonite churches, but in 1976 and 1979 we also had them in Ottawa. In 1976, Jake Epp, MP, hosted a fine dinner for them in the Parliamentary Restaurant. He was not available to do that in 1979 because at that time he was in cabinet, but MP John Reimer, joined by MPs Benno Friesen and Jake Froese, now extended the same hospitality. Among other things, these visitors asked the Canadian MPs how they reconciled their faith with membership in a political party; they also wanted to know how they were working for peace with the Soviet Union.

In 1979 we also included a visit to the Soviet Embassy. It turned out that the Embassy officials there were interested not only in these guests from their homeland but also in the people who had invited them, namely Mennonites of Canada. I responded by referring to our history; to MCC's various programs to help people in need in Canada and abroad, including our involvement in Vietnam and with the Palestinian people; to our conscientious objector stance; to our exchange programs committed to building people-to-people relations; and to our religiously rooted hope for peace.

After we left what had unexpectedly become a two-hour meeting at the Embassy, I apologized to the church delegates from the Soviet Union for having done so much of the talking. "Oh no," they responded, "what you said was just right; you gave those Embassy officials a very good picture of the church. The picture that our officials usually have, and in which they are trained, is very different and very narrow. That is why they are so hard on us. We have long tried to give them a broader picture of the church but with little success."

In addition to such exchange visits, there were individual concerns. Late in the 1960s, when Willi Brandt, Chancellor of West Germany, developed his "Ost-Politick", many people of German background who had moved to Russia in the eighteenth and nineteenth centuries were able to return to West Germany. This return movement included thousands of Mennonites. Some of them had close relatives in Canada. But would they be allowed to move from Germany to Canada? We made substantial inquiries, sometimes referring to the experience of Jewish people from the Soviet Union. Unfortunately, we were not able to work out a general arrangement.

A 1981 response from Minister Axworthy stated that "we will be pleased to examine individual cases as sympathetically as possible." And officials did help with some cases. In the mid-1980s, when the newly appointed Foreign Affairs minister, Joe Clark, made plans for an official visit to Moscow, he invited groups to submit cases for him to present to authorities there. This helped, but individual cases were never easy. Exit visas were hard to get and Canada's family reunification policies were narrowly defined.

When it was clear that a given individual would not be able to come, family members here looked for ways of sending help to them. On one occasion, in the mid-1980s, a woman from southern Ontario, intent on sending help to her brother in the Soviet Union, came to Ottawa. She had done some exploratory work on how to send aid, and we looked into the options further. Unfortunately, none of the options was guaranteed. In the end, she decided to pay for the purchase of a car for her brother, believing that he would be able to sell it and thus get the money. But would it really work? The uncertainty weighed on her. After she deposited the sizeable cheque, she said, sort of to me but more to herself: "I have done the best I can. I must now leave it with God."

10

OTHER INTERNATIONAL WORK

◆

The Canadian Foodgrains Bank
The Canadian Foodgrains Bank is now a very substantial organization, but in the summer of 1975 it was just an idea in the minds of a few people in Winnipeg, among them John Wieler, MCCC's Overseas Services Director. During one visit to Ottawa, he seemed to struggle with whether to move this idea forward and if so, then how. After listening to him for a while, I said I felt I could help him by fleshing out the idea in writing, which he could then present to others for formal consideration. John took me up on the offer, so I spent a full week in Winnipeg writing up certain basic documents while repeatedly checking with him to ensure that they reflected what he had in mind. That was in the era before computers, so the secretaries kindly typed and retyped the documents a number of times. We then reviewed them with other MCCers, including Art Defehr, who had recently completed a term in Bangladesh and had pressed John to pursue the idea.

When we had what seemed like a workable proposal, we met with representatives of what was then the Canadian Wheat Board. Also, I took the documents back to Ottawa to give to Tony Enns, a former MCCer who was now working in CIDA. He was most instrumental in persuading senior CIDA officials. Interestingly, on my flight from Winnipeg back to Ottawa, I noticed Otto Lang from Saskatchewan on the plane. He was the federal cabinet minister responsible for the Wheat Board. I could not pass up this opportunity to present the idea to him. He was very receptive. The fact that I could give him a written proposal was most helpful. It opened the door to direct communications with him and to getting the idea approved.

At that time the Food Bank, as it was then called, was an MCC initiative, but the intent was that if it proved workable then other church groups would be invited to join. After three years, that happened. It was renamed the Canadian Foodgrains Bank, and now its membership includes 15 church groups. In the total picture, my part was very small, but it may have helped to move the idea one step forward.

Somalia

Around 1980, MCC wanted to start a relief program in Somalia. There was widespread hunger, in part because of extensive fighting. We then arranged meetings for Ray Brubacher, director for Africa at MCC's head offices in Akron, Pennsylvania, to come and discuss plans with the Ambassador from Somalia. I then did considerable follow-up work with the Ambassador, because delivering aid in a situation of conflict was complicated. As much as possible MCC wanted the food aid to be distributed to people on all sides, because they all needed food and also because of MCC's hope for an eventual reconciliation. The Ambassador's interest developed quickly. Soon he asked that we double and triple our program there. He also wanted us to get more Canadian NGOs to send relief and to persuade the Canadian government to be more generous. The Canadian Foodgrains Bank did become active, organizing a sizeable "Corn for the Horn" campaign to raise donations. But the Canadian government at that time had significant reservations about the Somali government.

In 1985, we went to the Ambassador with a different request. Two

Somali individuals who had been convicted of stealing from MCC workers in Somalia were to be executed. MCC was concerned about this, both because of its basic opposition to capital punishment and because of how their execution for stealing from a western Christian organization might be viewed. As I worked on this matter, I learned of another plea for mercy. In 1962, a Mennonite missionary from Ontario, Merlin Grove, was stabbed to death in Somalia while he was registering students for a new school term. The attacker was to be executed, but the Grove family and the other missionaries had pleaded that his life be spared, which it then was.

That stance of the Mennonites, together with their approach in general, led to an amazing goodwill. Some Somalis began to refer to themselves as Muslim Mennonites. Some years later, when the conflicts in Somalia forced the missionaries to withdraw and many Somali people to flee, a good number settled in Ontario. Some of them now looked up Mennonites and remarkable friendships developed. In the early 1990s the Canadian Somali Friendship Association for Peace was formed with a former Mennonite missionary and a Somali Muslim as co-chairs. In 2010 when Dorothy Grove, the widow of Merlin, died, several dozen Somali Muslims from the Toronto area came to the funeral.

Iran
When a major earthquake hit Iran in June 1990, MCC's overseas directors wanted to respond. One reason was the basic MCC desire to alleviate human need. But MCC was also interested in exploring the possibility of a longer-term involvement, given that Iran had been closed to Westerners since the 1979 Islamic revolution. Unlike the US, Canada had diplomatic relations with Iran, having resumed them in 1988, albeit at a low level. For this reason, MCC asked me to approach the Iranian representative in Ottawa about shipping relief supplies. It turned out that the Iranian representative, a young man very new to his responsibilities, had to do considerable searching before he could respond. To do this, I had to help him understand MCC and the Mennonite people. This led to extensive

Other International Work

and interesting discussions. But it did not take too long before the shipping and distribution plans were in place.

In the following years our relations with the Iranian representatives in Ottawa played a significant role as MCC increased its involvement. MCC sent delegations to visit Iran, stationed workers there, arranged for Iranian university students to spend a year or two in Canadian institutions, involved Mennonite theologians in extended inter-faith dialogue with Shia Muslim scholars, etc. The Canadian government, however, remained quite cool towards Iran, citing its human rights record, including its oppression of the Ba'hai minority, its attitude toward Israel, and its nuclear program. Nor was there much interest from other Canadian NGOs. This meant that we in MCC were relatively alone in this involvement. (Thus, we received quite a few invitations to receptions and dinners from the Iranian diplomats.)

In 2007 one Iranian diplomat in Ottawa asked if we would consider hosting a dialogue where senior Iranian officials could interact directly with their Canadian counterparts. He felt this might open the way to better relations. What would be the subject of such a dialogue? The diplomat was open, but from the Canadian perspective Iran's nuclear program was clearly a concern. Could we make that the subject of a conference? He was open to that. We then decided to approach Ernie Regehr of Project Ploughshares, who had extensive connections with Canadian experts in this field. Ernie and I then approached Canadian government officials; they seemed interested and sympathetic, so we kept them "in the loop" as we planned the conference.

In the end, the Canadian officials did not participate in this gathering. However, several Canadian scholars and a number of retired diplomats were keen. Peter Jones of the University of Ottawa provided the venue and facilities. And the people sent by Iran represented its side well. The conference, in the spring of 2008, was challenging, but everyone seemed pleased to be able to talk about the issues. I do not claim that it contributed to the big-power negotiations that led to the 2015 agreement with Iran, but I do not doubt that it was worth doing. Unfortunately, Canada cut off diplomatic relations with Iran in 2012. Since then, its embassy in downtown Ottawa has been closed.

A Generous CIDA Official
The Canadian government, through CIDA, had long provided funding to non-governmental organizations like MCC for development work in "third world" countries. At first the funding was given on a matching basis for specific projects, but later MCCC received block grants for five-year periods, although these required detailed planning, reporting, and evaluation. I was not involved in that interaction in an ongoing way. But one day in the later 1990s, near the end of the government's fiscal year, a CIDA official with whom I had had some difficult dealings called with regard to a community level conflict resolution centre in the Middle East that both he and I had visited. MCC had long provided modest support for that centre but it needed more. Now this official said that if it still needed money, he might be able to make a special grant, but I would have to get a proposal to him within 48 hours!

Naturally, I dropped everything else and got on the phone to the centre in the Middle East and asked for reports and plans, all of which came by fax. (We did not yet use email.) This CIDA official said he might be able to help the centre's budget for two years and urged me not to skimp. When I then brought the proposal to him, he took one look and told me to rewrite it and ask for more, to increase each line so that in reality it covered the center for three years even though for CIDA purposes it still had to appear as two years. Clearly, the CIDA official wanted to get certain funds moved out before the fiscal year ended. We then had to persuade some other officials, but soon everyone agreed and the center was helped in a most exceptional way. To this day, I have a small olive wood plaque from that conflict resolution centre above my desk.

11

Canadian Constitutional Reform

◆

From the 1960s to the 1990s, there was extensive discussion about changing Canada's Constitution, particularly on whether to accommodate the concerns of Quebec in a better way. We worked on this issue on two occasions.

The Initiative of Pierre Trudeau
In the decade of the 1970s, Prime Minister Pierre Trudeau made several attempts at constitutional reform. These were not successful, but when he was returned to power in 1980 he approached this issue with a new determination. He now brought forward a Charter of Rights and Freedoms which quickly became the focus of discussion. A Special Joint Committee of Members of the House of Commons and of the Senate was authorized to hold hearings on it. I prepared a submission for this committee and then, thanks to MP Jake Epp, MCCC was invited to appear before it on November 25, 1980.

With me were Ross Nigh, then chair of Mennonite Central Committee Canada, and J. M. Klassen, the Executive Director. We addressed two concerns. One was conscientious objection. The Charter, as proposed, stated simply that "Everyone has ... freedom of conscience and religion." We asked for a phrase to protect "conscientious objection to the taking of human life", explaining that this would apply to military service as well as to police work and medical practices such as euthanasia and abortion. We reviewed the long history of provisions for conscientious objection to military service and, with regard to abortion, we referred to the government's own Badgley Report of 1977.

Though the discussion was sympathetic, our proposal was not accepted. However, in a follow-up letter, dated February 3, 1981, the then Minister of Justice, the Hon. Jean Chrétien, stated:

> I believe that the Charter as it is presently drafted could provide the protections you request.... I believe that 'freedom of conscience' as provided in Section 2(a) is sufficiently broad to be interpreted by the courts to permit conscientious objection. Also, as your submission to the Special Joint Committee points out, the exemption accorded to the Mennonites and others has been respected over the years, to the extent possible, without constitutional protection.

The second concern that we brought forward was that the provision for freedom of religion in "Everyone has ... freedom of ... religion ..." was too individualistic and that "there are occasions when we would see it as right that the freedom of individuals be restricted for the sake of the freedom of a community." To support this, we referred to the 1970 Supreme Court decision that Hutterite colonies were not obligated to give to individuals who left a colony "their share" of the colony's assets. We also noted the government's decision to exempt Amish and Old Order Mennonites, as well as Hutterites, from the Canada Pension Plan even though, arguably, such an exemption left individuals more dependent on the group. The Committee gave us a good hearing. We felt we were able to respond well to their questions. In the end the Committee did not accept the new wording that we proposed.

Canadian Constitutional Reform

The Initiatives of Brian Mulroney

Late in the 1980s, Prime Minister Brian Mulroney launched a new round of constitutional discussions. The Quebec government had never joined in adopting the 1981 constitutional package of which the Charter was a key part. Mulroney wanted to make the necessary changes so that Quebec would sign on. He was encouraged by the fact that Quebec now had a sympathetic premier in Robert Bourassa. Mulroney made two momentous efforts. The first involved the Meech Lake Accord. It was accepted by all the provincial premiers in 1987 but in the following three years, during which it was to be approved by each of the eleven legislatures, some objections emerged. In the end, it did not quite get the required approval.

The second Mulroney effort involved the Charlottetown Accord, adopted by the premiers in August 1992. This was more complex. In addition to addressing the place of Quebec in Canada, it also had provisions for the Aboriginal people; indeed, several aboriginal groups were involved in the negotiations. Some of their concerns referred to the "group rights" idea that we had raised in our earlier submission.

The Mulroney government wanted to have the Charlottetown Accord ratified in a national referendum. This led to widespread public discussion. In this context, the MCCC Executive Committee asked me to write a paper on the issue. I presented this paper, entitled "Supporting Canadian Constitutional Reform: A Discussion Paper Issued by MCCC," to the full board at its annual meeting in January 1992. It was not a submission for the government; its purpose was to facilitate discussion in our churches in relation to the forthcoming referendum.

In general my paper was sympathetic to the Charlottetown Accord. It drew on Biblical material as well as the experience of Mennonite and Brethren in Christ people and other countries to show that minority groups had been accommodated in various ways. The paper concluded that "there should be greater accommodation of Quebec's concerns" as well as "a fuller acceptance of the claims of the Aboriginal people."

Two developments at that 1992 annual meeting of MCCC may have influenced the board toward approving this paper. One was the participation of Sonia Blanchette from the Mennonite Brethren churches in Quebec. She said, to the surprise of board members, that Quebec's separation from Canada was "only a matter of time" and that a good number of Quebec Mennonites were sympathetic to the sovereigntist cause. The other development was the acknowledgement that that year, 1992, was the 500th anniversary of legendary voyage by Christopher Columbus and the European "discovery" of North America, and that this had had devastating consequences for indigenous peoples. Both of these developments suggested that minorities should be accommodated, if possible.

Soon thereafter, MCCC printed the paper as a pamphlet and sent it out to the churches. I received positive feedback from a number of individuals, but the mood in many churches and in the country generally was ambivalent. When the referendum was held, in October 1992, the Charlottetown Accord was narrowly rejected, despite being supported in Quebec. This rejection in "English" Canada is generally seen as a key reason why the separatist Parti Quebecois was returned to power in Quebec's 1994 election. The following year it held a referendum on sovereignty and came very close to winning. In later years, however, the sovereigntist cause lost much of its support.

If my memory is correct then, in 1980, we were the only church organization to make a submission to the Parliamentary Committee on the Charter of Rights and Freedoms. In the early 1990s, when the Charlottetown Accord was being considered, a number of national church groups entered the discussion. As far as I know, they all expressed support.

12

WAR CRIMINALS

◆

Soon after the Mulroney government was elected in 1984, it took steps to fulfill its election promise of acting against war criminals who might have found their way to Canada. One of the men in question was Mr. Jacob Luitjens from the Netherlands. He had collaborated with the Nazi forces that occupied his country during WW II. When the war ended in 1945, he gave himself up to the authorities and was sent to prison to await trial. After two reportedly very difficult years in prison, he escaped, and in the summer of 1948, using the name Gerhard Harder, he managed to get on a ship carrying Mennonite refugees to Paraguay. His mother had been Mennonite.

Soon after arriving in Paraguay, Luitjens had a religious conversion. He then accepted baptism and started to use his original name, Luitjens, again. Also, he married and became a beloved high school teacher in a Mennonite colony. In 1961, he and his wife moved to British Columbia following his wife's parents. He soon joined a Mennonite church there and after further studies became a university science lecturer. Meanwhile, in the Netherlands, in 1948 he had been tried in absentia and convicted of "deliberately aiding and abetting the enemy in time of war." There were claims that, as part of that "aiding and abetting," he had killed two individuals, but the Dutch court held that that was not proven. His sentence was life in prison.

Our Early Involvement, 1985
The first stage of our involvement took place in 1985. Luitjens had already been in the news earlier. In 1980 a man who had fought in the Dutch Resistance visited BC and happened to notice his name. He then contacted the Dutch government, which then requested that Luitjens be extradited. The Canadian government refused this request on the ground that the extradition treaty with the Netherlands did not cover "collaboration with the enemy in time of war." But now, with the Mulroney government's new initiative, it was assumed that sooner or later Luitjens would be affected. Because of that, a minister at the Mennonite church in BC where he was a member wrote to MCCC and asked that we intervene. At its meeting in March 1985, the MCCC Executive Committee asked me to prepare a paper on the issue and offer advice.

My aim in writing that paper was to find a way of integrating the principles of justice and accountability with those of mercy and forgiveness. I then consulted with church leaders and theologians at several Mennonite colleges. On one occasion when Sol Littman, a prominent Jewish leader, addressed an audience in Ottawa, I took the opportunity in the Question and Answer period to ask if he saw any room for forgiveness in dealing with war criminals. I explained that I was not thinking of mass murderers like Adolf Eichmann but rather of someone whose crimes were relatively minor, who might not have killed anyone, and who had, in his subsequent life, demonstrated a repentant spirit by contributing to human well-being as opportunities had allowed. Could there be any mercy for such a person? Littman replied with a strong affirmative, adding that if there were any such people, they would be very few. Still, the fact that he affirmed the idea gave me a basic principle that I felt could be used for looking at the case of Luitjens.

When I presented my paper to the MCCC Executive Committee in late August 1985, they asked that I seek a meeting with the government's newly created War Crimes Commission and that Siegfried Bartel, a member of the MCCC Executive Committee, join me in that meeting. Mr. Bartel, now a firm pacifist, had been an officer in the German army during WW II but had immigrated to Canada after the war and settled in BC. We were granted a meeting with Michael Meighen and Yves Fortier, the two lawyers for the Commission. It took place on October 31, 1985. I explained that we did not deny or minimize the Holocaust or the other suffering that the Nazis had caused and that we did not come with suggestions for dealing with mass murderers, but that we felt that for some individuals the idea of mercy could still be considered.

Then Siegfried, drawing on his personal experience and speaking with deep conviction, said war makes people do such terrible things that those who come later, in times of peace, should be very cautious about how they judge; that many soldiers on all sides had done things that were morally worse than what Luitjens was accused of, even though technically they might not have been illegal. To illustrate this point he referred to the fire-bombing of Dresden by the Allies. Then he talked about forgiveness, mentioning several very difficult situations where forgiveness had been extended. He concluded that if we want to survive as human beings, then we have to take our guidance from the line in the Lord's Prayer about "forgiving others as we want to be forgiven." The meeting went well beyond the scheduled half-hour; the two lawyers responded with warm appreciation, indicating considerable sympathy with our general concern but on the case of Luitjens, they intimated that there might be more in the file than we were aware of.

Earlier in the fall, after the MCCC Executive Committee had accepted my paper, it became a public document. I then shared it with people whose input had helped me in writing it. The *Mennonite Reporter* then carried a front-page story that lifted up the justice and accountability dimension somewhat more than the mercy and forgiveness side, probably because the editors felt that Mennonites needed to be challenged in that area. That prompted considerable discussion in Mennonite circles. A majority of the voices wanted

MCCC to argue primarily for mercy and forgiveness. Some spoke from having lived through the horrors of WW II in Europe; others felt that the Christian message can only be one of forgiveness regardless of the circumstance; still others held that surely Luitjens would have confessed to whatever wrongs he had committed when he sought baptism in a Mennonite church in Paraguay, and that the church in Canada should now accept that as closing the matter. Some pointed out that while Canada had supported the prosecution of the major war criminals soon after WW II, no Canadian government, of either party, had pursued the "small players," and that we should urge the current government to continue with that approach. Only a few spoke about the need for accountability.

Later Developments, 1986 – 1993

After the War Crimes Commission completed its work, the government brought in new legislation. The first plan was to hold trials in Canada on the substance of the charges for any suspected individuals. This was to protect them from questionable evidence that might be deemed acceptable in some foreign courts but not in Canadian courts. (The Canadian Ukrainian Congress had pressed for this because they did not want Canadian Ukrainians to have to appear before a court in what was then the Soviet Union.) This approach of having trials in Canada ran into legal problems, so the government resorted to looking at how suspected individuals had obtained Canadian immigration and citizenship papers; specifically, had they been truthful in answering all the questions? This became the focus of the legal proceedings against Luitjens which began in 1988. The proceedings continued for several years, but late in 1992 he was deported to the Netherlands.

When the government began the process of revoking his citizenship, on April 18, 1988 we prepared a letter for the Minister of Justice, Ramon Hnatyshyn. We referred to the conversation with Sol Littman, noting that what it implied was comparable to the discretion that judges and prosecutors often exercised when they decided on how to deal with particular cases. We acknowledged that our information about what Luitjens did during the war might be incomplete but we had strong grounds for saying that he had a repentant spirit. We noted that he had been a beloved teacher both in Paraguay and in Canada, that he had renounced his wartime actions and loyalties, and that his decision to again use his original name suggested that he had not tried to conceal his past. In his response of June 28, 1988, Mr. Hnatyshyn said, "I ... very much regret not being able to reply more fully to your letter particularly since I appreciate its balanced and considerate approach. However, I cannot comment on a case ... before the court."

Even before we wrote to Hnatyshyn, the Conference of Mennonites in Canada (CMC), predecessor of Mennonite Church Canada, sent a sharply worded letter to him on March 24. They said, "We are ... calling on you to do everything in your power to have these charges dropped"; further, "The action being taken by the Government seems selective and vindictive.... It almost appears as though the Government feels that it must be seen to be taking some action ... and is using Mr. Luitjens as a convenient 'pawn' in this effort to placate some of the strident voices calling for vengeance...."

Taking a very different view, Mennonites in the Netherlands now wrote to the CMC about how harmful Luitjens' wartime actions had been, that people were terrorized. "Justice would mean," wrote the General Secretary of the Dutch Mennonites, that "these people have the right to find that ... our society recognizes that they were wronged, ... if Mr. Luitjens is, indeed, guilty of minor crimes only, then that too should be made clear." He "should come home to the place where the truth of his life and of other people's lives lie and either accept the sentence or ask for a reopening of the case...."

In 1991 the highly respected J. M. Klassen, Executive Director Emeritus of MCCC, was travelling in Europe. He took the opportunity to meet with two Dutch Mennonite leaders. He reported: "I challenged [them] about ... what the Dutch Mennonites were willing to do. Were they willing to bear the reproach of an 'erring' brother Mennonite? Was it right for them to disown him?

Were they afraid ... to be seen in a less favourable light by their own government? Would they be willing to be a pastor to Luitjens if he is returned to Holland so that he is assured of their love and support while he takes his punishment? Could the Dutch Mennonites not take upon themselves Luitjens' reproach and attempt to mediate with the victims?"

The Federal Court of Canada, which heard the case in the spring of 1989, received testimony from witnesses from the Netherlands about the charges against Luitjens. He denied many of the details. Whether he had been entirely truthful about his past when he applied for Canadian immigration and citizenship status could not be established definitively because the government had not kept those records. However, the court concluded that he had not. On this basis, and after further judicial proceedings, he was deported to the Netherlands late in 1992. There he was taken to prison, where he was kept until March 1995. When the Dutch government announced his release, it noted his age as well as the fact that other "collaborators" had been released early, and, further, that Luitjens had been a model prisoner in every way. He then lived out his years in a small village in the Netherlands, where he kept to himself. Canada would not let him come back but his wife, who remained a Canadian citizen, returned often to visit their children.

Concluding Thoughts on the War Criminals Issue

It was a challenging issue. There were so many views and arguments, most of which had some validity. Several times, I was invited to meet with Jewish leaders who wanted me to understand their perspective. For its part, MCC in British Columbia, being close to Mr. Luitjens and his church and having many post-WW II immigrants close by, felt the issue keenly and struggled hard. A number of times they asked me for legal analyses and updates. Several MPs from British Columbia also asked for our views, as did people from various churches.

Obviously, many things would have been easier if our involvement had begun earlier, before Luitjens was even noticed by the government. Maybe then, with the right kind of support, he would have been willing to voluntarily return to the Netherlands and accept the consequences. His brother-in-law, who had moved to Paraguay but not to Canada, had done that, as had others. Then, after a time in prison they resumed life in the Netherlands. According to Peter J. Dyck, the veteran MCC leader who helped many Mennonites from Europe to get to Paraguay after WW II, Luitjens had indicated interest in exploring that option at one point. Later, Peter deeply regretted that he had not taken time to discuss it with Luitjens and to try to 'walk with him'. If that route had been taken, how long would he have been kept in prison in the Netherlands, and would Canada have allowed him back in after his release? We don't know.

Did all our advocacy make a difference? Perhaps not in terms of what happened to Jacob Luitjens. But it led to extensive interaction with all kinds of people and also to deeper reflection on important issues: about how to actually combine justice and mercy; about how to support a repentant wrong-doer while also respecting those who were wronged; about what it means to be an international church; about the wounds of war that continue long after the guns have gone silent, and other things. Since Luitjens was a member of a Mennonite church, it is inevitable that Mennonite people would express their views on these and related questions during the course of the proceedings. Our involvement made us somewhat of a focal point.

13

Abortion

◆

The abortion issue was widely debated during the first decades of the MCC Ottawa Office. Every political party had people on both sides of it. A 1969 change in the Criminal Code had made abortions legal if, in the opinion of the three doctors on a hospital's therapeutic abortion committee, the continuation of the pregnancy was likely to endanger the woman's life or health.

In the years after the 1969 change, the number of reported abortions rose rapidly. This led to a range of questions: how were doctors on therapeutic abortion committees interpreting the word "health"; were hospitals obligated to set up therapeutic abortion committees and thus provide access to abortion services; should special abortion clinics be allowed; should medical workers have conscientious objector rights; and so on. There were major lobbying campaigns, court challenges, and Private Members' bills in Parliament. Many church groups wrestled with the issue.

Like many organizations, MCCC was not completely of one mind on it. The statements adopted by MCCC's member denominations were generally pro-life, as were the Members of Parliament from Mennonite areas. In the Ottawa Office, we monitored developments and reported on them through our usual channels. When we drafted general letters for new Prime Ministers, we referred to this issue alongside MCCC's other concerns. To illustrate, the January 22,

Abortion

1980 letter addressed to the Rt. Hon. Joe Clark, stated:

> Seventhly, we want to express our concern on the issue of abortion. We recognize it to be sensitive and difficult in particular ways. Yet the current official number of 60,000 per year is very sobering. We believe that all parts of our society, including government, the medical professions, counselling agencies, educational institutions, the communication media and not least of all the families and the churches must look for better ways and do much more to reduce abortions and to promote greater respect for all of life.

In 1981 we helped in drafting the MCCC pamphlet "The Problem of Abortion: A Service Response," to encourage people and congregations to support local groups seeking to provide practical support to pregnant women in difficult situations. The January 30, 1985 letter to newly elected Prime Minister Brian Mulroney said: "We have long been involved with a modest program giving various kinds of practical assistance to pregnant women in difficult situations.... We do not expect government by itself to solve the problem completely but we want to encourage you to look for ways to help our society to deal with it in a better way than is presently the case."

In 1988 the debate changed. On January 28 of that year, the Supreme Court ruled that the existing law, specifically the requirement that the approval of therapeutic abortion committees was needed, violated the Charter of Rights and Freedoms. However, the Court also indicated that a different law, providing some protection for the fetus, might still be acceptable. Now, churches and organizations wrestled with the issue anew. Many Mennonites were concerned. We then prepared a February 18 letter for MCCC that stated in part:

> In our view ... action is needed both from governments and from non-governmental organizations. As a church group, we wish to strengthen our commitment to a

service response ... as outlined in the enclosed brochure .... In addition, we want to urge the government to act. The Supreme Court, while overturning the existing law, indicated that a new law providing certain protections for the unborn might nevertheless be upheld. We believe this should be urgently explored.... Social and economic support programs are also needed to ensure that people are not pressured to seek abortions by the prospect of poverty....

In the summer of 1988, the Mulroney government considered introducing a bill with a "gestational approach," meaning that the law might prohibit abortions at the later stages of pregnancy but not at the earlier stages. This approach was suggested by the Law Reform Commission but found little support in Parliament. After the election in November 1988, the Mulroney government made a stronger attempt but with a different approach. Both MP John Reimer, who was on the committee of the Progressive Conservative caucus charged with formulating an approach, and Jake Epp, who was in the cabinet, favoured a "grounds approach," meaning that abortions would be prohibited except for certain grounds, e.g., if the continuation of the pregnancy might endanger the woman's life or health. They opposed a gestational approach because, in Epp's words, "if we ever accept the principle that life somehow gains value as it matures, we are then subject to that greater danger of asking ... does life lose value as it ages?" Perhaps, he was thinking of euthanasia.

In the summer of 1989 there were several high profile court cases and extensive public discussion about the government's anticipated initiative. The Executive Committee of MCCC was scheduled to meet in mid-September, so we prepared a letter for the Prime Minister. It recommended more social support for pregnant women facing poverty or other hardships, as well as education campaigns to promote respect for life somewhat the way the government was urging people not to smoke tobacco. Regarding the law, we

Abortion

expressed support for a "grounds" approach defined quite narrowly. We also asked that the law include "conscientious objector" rights for medical personnel. The MCCC Executive Committee approved the letter, although some members of the Committee said they would have preferred to allow only one "ground," namely where the life of the mother was at risk. Once the letter was approved, we sent copies to all Members of Parliament. To my surprise, our letter was then carried in full in the publications of the four largest MCCC member denominations: the *Mennonite Reporter*, the *Mennonite Brethren Herald*, *The EMC Messenger*, and *The EMMC Recorder*.

In November 1989 the government introduced its bill, number C-43. It was remarkably simple. It prohibited abortions but included a notable exception, namely, where one doctor stated that the continuation of the pregnancy posed a danger to the woman's life or health. And health could be defined very broadly so as to allow for almost any aspect of human well-being. People like Epp and Reimer had hoped for a stronger pro-life bill but there was opposition to that within the Progressive Conservative caucus. Nevertheless, they defended the bill, saying that it established a principle, namely a prohibition on abortions. However, critics on the pro-life side, who were as vociferous as critics on the pro-choice side, said that the exception was so broad as to render it almost meaningless. Epp tried hard to address these and other concerns as, for example, in his November 21, 1989 speech in the House of Commons. In May 1990 the bill passed in the House but only by nine votes. When it got to the Senate early in 1991, the vote ended in a tie, meaning that the bill died. Since then there has been no comparable effort to pass a law. Politics and government often involve efforts to accommodate opposing views. In this instance it was not to be.

14

CONSCIENTIOUS OBJECTION

◆

Conscientious Objection and Citizenship Law

When MCC set up the Ottawa Office in 1975, protection for conscientious objection was almost a non-issue. There was no conscription; Canada was not at war; and many other issues were pressing. Nevertheless, given the issue's longstanding importance for Mennonites, it was natural that we would work on it if a need or opportunity arose. The first such opportunity arose in the fall of 1976 when my friend and former law professor, Ian A. Hunter, called me about how Thorbjorn and Bente Jensen, immigrants from Denmark, had been refused citizenship.

Hunter had seen a newspaper story about what happened. In 1973 a citizenship judge, using the provision in the law that says that applicants for citizenship should have an adequate understanding of the privileges and responsibilities of citizenship, had asked the Jensens how they understood those responsibilities in the event of war. When the Jensens, being Jehovah's Witnesses, had explained that they would not bear arms, the judge ruled that they did not meet the qualifications for citizenship. In 1976 the Jensens' case was heard by a Citizenship Appeal Court judge who upheld the earlier ruling. Upon hearing of this Hunter, contacted me to ask if MCC might want to take up the cause; if so, he stood ready to provide his legal services.

I then contacted the Jensens, who lived in Belleville, Ontario, and Hunter contacted his law school friend, John I. Laskin. At first Hunter and Laskin attempted to appeal the decision to a higher court but when obstacles to this course appeared, Hunter wrote a lengthy letter (November 11, 1976) to the responsible Minister, John Roberts, outlining the legal situation and asking for a meeting with him. Roberts agreed to the meeting, set for a wintry morning in Ottawa. As it happened bad weather made him late, so we had some free time with the two officials whom he had asked to participate in the meeting. We learned quickly that they were not sympathetic. They argued that if the Jensens made another application, they would probably be approved because in all likelihood they would come before a different judge who would not ask them this question. Also, since the Jensens had landed immigrant status, they had the right to continue living in Canada even if they were not citizens.

We, however, wanted to have the law state clearly that people could not be denied citizenship on the grounds of conscientious objection. (In the years after World War II, several Mennonite immigrants had been denied citizenship for the same reason.) After presenting our arguments to the Minister, he indicated that he would consider our request and get back to us. Then, on the way out of his office, he asked John Laskin if he was related to the highly respected Bora Laskin, then Chief Justice of the Supreme Court. "Yes, he's my Dad," was John's response. A few days later I received a proposal from one of the officials indicating their plan to include a provision in the Regulations under the Citizenship Act to say that if an applicant was a conscientious objector by reason of his religion, then the judge would not be allowed to ask how he understood his citizenship responsibilities in relation to war.

We would have preferred a provision in the Act itself, but we and the Jensens were happy for this. Our timing was fortunate. The officials were just then preparing a whole new body of regulations to accompany the new Act that Parliament had recently passed but which had not yet come into force. Incorporating one more idea in the regulations was not difficult. The Minister's discovery about

John Laskin's father will not have hurt our cause.

Soon thereafter, MP Jake Epp, with whom I had discussed this matter, introduced a Private Member's bill that would have inserted a broader definition of conscientious objection into the Citizenship Act, thereby giving it a firmer basis. Unfortunately, like most Private Members' bills, this one did not become law.

When we began this effort, we thought there might be an expensive court process, so I approached the national Jehovah's Witness body about cost-sharing possibilities. They were grateful for MCC's effort but they declined to provide funding, explaining that the issue did not affect their right to witness and minister. Fortunately, John Laskin and Ian Hunter charged us only for their travel expenses.

Hunter wrote an article about this development for the *Dalhousie Law Journal* of May 1978. Years later, after retiring from teaching, he became, among other things, an occasional columnist in the *National Post* and the *Globe and Mail*. Laskin became a judge on the Federal Court of Appeal.

In 1999, when a House of Commons Committee studied a bill for a new Citizenship Act (Bill C – 63), we appeared before it and, among other things, asked that the word "defend" in the Oath of Citizenship be changed to the word "uphold," as in the phrase, "I promise to ... uphold our democratic values, ..." The Committee accepted our proposal, but the bill died on the Order paper when a general election was called.

Other Conscientious Objector Developments
In the early 1980s, when the apartheid regime in South Africa was still firmly in place, some young white men felt they could not serve in their military forces. However, South Africa's laws had no provisions for conscientious objectors, so these men either went into exile or served prison sentences which included repeated periods of solitary confinement. MCC workers from the region became acquainted with some of these men. One such MCCer was Ron Mathies. When he and his family were on home leave, early

in 1982, he came to Ottawa together with Richard Steele, a South African who had been in prison there. We arranged meetings for them with several MPs and External Affairs officials.

Obviously the situation of conscientious objectors was only a small aspect of the broader apartheid situation in South Africa, but it was supported by church groups and others in the US and Europe. Canadian government representatives were quite open on it too, perhaps because it was an issue to which they could respond without challenging South Africa's basic structures. Thus, External Affairs officials agreed to communicate with South African authorities about accommodating CO's, using Canada's history with CO provisions as an example. Likewise, MP Jake Epp appealed to officials at the South African Embassy in Ottawa. And we provided them with background information. Our contributions were small in the total picture, but in 1983 South African authorities changed their laws so as to provide at least some accommodation for conscientious objectors.

A very different issue came up in the early 1990s. A young man, Brian Palmer, who had voluntarily enlisted in the Canadian military in 1987, had then developed conscientious objector convictions, primarily from reading the New Testament. He had then asked to be discharged on these grounds. Since there were no regulations or policies for dealing with such requests, he had been re-assigned to non-combatant duties for the remainder of his three-year commitment. After completing those three years, he approached us about the issue.

This happened soon after the 1991 Gulf War. In the build-up towards that war, MCC workers in Europe had received several hundred inquiries from American service personnel at a nearby US military base. They had asked for information on how to apply for a discharge from the military on grounds of conscience. Fortunately, US military regulations allowed for such a discharge, although it was not a simple process. That the US had such regulations helped us to make our request of the Canadian military.

We made our request in a letter dated March 26, 1991,

addressed to the Minister of Justice and the Minister of Defence. Interestingly, eight other church groups officially endorsed our letter: the Canadian Council of Churches, the Evangelical Fellowship of Canada, the United Church of Canada, the Canadian Yearly Meeting of the Religious Society of Friends (Quakers), the Evangelical Lutheran Church in Canada, the Pentecostal Assemblies of Canada, the Seventh-Day Adventist Church in Canada, and the Union of Spiritual Communities of Christ (Orthodox Doukhobors).

The Defence Department showed significant openness but things moved slowly. In April 1992 we met with Defence officials. Our delegation included Brian Palmer as well as Quaker representatives. Now officials indicated that they were in the process of revising their regulations to ensure that they complied with new Human Rights policies and that they might be able to incorporate our request in this process.

Late in 1995, after other communications, the Defence Department stated that they had granted an "in principle" approval to our request. They sent us a draft of the regulations they were preparing. We suggested a number of revisions, many of which were accepted.

15

OTHER SOCIAL ISSUES

◆

Tobacco Advertising Restrictions
It is hard to recall the time when smoking was common and cigarette advertising widespread. Already in the early 1980s, opposition to these practices had reached the point where cigarette advertising on television and radio was prohibited. In the fall of 1987, Jake Epp, now Minister of Health, introduced a bill that would go further: it would also ban tobacco advertising on billboards and magazines, forbid tobacco companies from sponsoring sports or cultural events, and ban smoking in all federal government office buildings.

There was considerable public debate about this bill: tobacco companies said that jobs in their factories would be lost; newspapers and magazines said they would lose advertising revenue and might have to close; and cultural institutions like the Royal Winnipeg Ballet, which had long benefitted from being sponsored by the Imperial Tobacco Company, made the same point. For his part, Jake Epp argued that 35,000 Canadians died from smoking-related causes every year and that the health care and related costs exceeded $7 billion.

For us in MCC, it was unusually easy to respond to this issue since smoking had never enjoyed much support among Mennonites. We then prepared a letter arguing that "a ban on advertising was a minimal response", that the prohibitions on what advertising tobacco companies could do in Canada should be extended to their advertising abroad, particularly in third-world countries where they were expanding their marketing efforts, and that the government should consider enacting similar prohibitions on the advertising of alcohol. The MCCC chairperson, Ray Brubacher, signed the letter and we then sent it to every Member of Parliament. Many other groups also supported Epp's initiative.

Pornography and Violence against Women
In 1990, when there were reports that the Mulroney government might be open to taking certain actions on pornography, I was asked by individuals in the Canadian Conference of Catholic Bishops (CCCB) and the Evangelical Fellowship of Canada (EFC) to chair a meeting of representatives from various church groups to explore the possibility of joint advocacy on this and related issues.

A good number of church groups were interested. After several meetings we prepared a joint letter to the Minister of Justice stating that "We are agreed that the production, distribution and exhibition of pornography 1) involving children and 2) depicting violent or degrading behaviour in a sexual context should be offences under the Criminal Code." We then listed ten reasons supporting this view and expressed interest in further discussions with officials. The letter was signed by senior representatives of the CCCB, the EFC, the United, Anglican, Presbyterian, Christian Reformed, and Salvation Army churches, as well as by leaders of MCC and the Women's Inter-Church Council. We also prepared a letter specifically for MCC. Signed by MCCC chair Ray Brubacher and addressed to the Minister of Justice, it said: "We believe there is a substantial need to restrain the production and sale of visual sexual depictions that include violence, involve children, or otherwise seriously misrepresent the gift of sexuality." The MCC office in Winnipeg also urged the leaders of its member conferences to communicate their support for the recommended actions directly to the government.

Regarding violence against women specifically, in 1991 the

government announced a "Blue Ribbon" panel to study this matter. Our inter-church group then asked Jennifer Leddy from the CCCB, Joy Kennedy from the Anglicans, and me to prepare a submission. We entitled it "And No One Shall Make Them Afraid," a phrase from Micah 4:4 in the Bible. It was approved by all the church groups mentioned above whose representatives then presented to the government's blue ribbon panel. Seeing the eager support for this common action from such a range of churches was very satisfying. We then printed this submission as a pamphlet. A number of the church bodies then used that pamphlet to promote awareness of the issues in their own denominations.

Divorce

In January 1984 the Minister of Justice, Mark MacGuigan, introduced a bill to change Canada's divorce law. The existing law allowed divorce on a range of grounds including adultery, physical or mental cruelty, conviction of a sexual offence, or marriage breakdown. This last ground was assumed to have been met if a couple had lived separately for three years.

The 1984 proposal would cut that three-year separation requirement to one year. If someone wanted a divorce even more quickly, they could still go to court and prove certain grounds but most people preferred to simply wait out the one-year separation. This made it unnecessary to go through the process of proving that one spouse was at fault; hence, the term "no-fault" divorce. The 1984 proposal also stipulated that the custody of children should be determined by the best interests of the children, not by who was at fault for the marriage difficulties. The bill also proposed changes in how support and maintenance orders should be arranged.

Should MCCC make a response to this proposal? The Executive Committee asked me to make a recommendation. In order to do so, I wrote to 15 leaders of various Mennonite groups. Many of them responded in remarkably thoughtful ways. In the end, we in MCCC did not submit a response to the government. However, I wrote a sizeable piece for the Mennonite papers in Canada, describing the government's proposals and noting various pros and cons. Then I urged people to express their views to their Members of Parliament.

Significantly, Mr. MacGuigan's proposal died on the order paper when the 1984 election was called. That election brought Brian Mulroney to power. In 1986 his government brought in changes to the divorce law that were quite similar to those proposed by MacGuigan.

Gun Control

The Montreal Massacre of December 6, 1989, when 14 female engineering students were killed, prompted many calls for gun control. Before long, the Coalition for Gun Control was formed. Five months after the massacre, the Minister of Justice, Kim Campbell, introduced a bill to ban certain kinds of guns and to strengthen the screening requirements for others. The bill was supported by the Canadian Police Association but was defeated in the House of Commons. In May 1991, Campbell tried again, with Bill C – 17. It went further than the previous bill, and now a broad range of groups favouring gun control were prepared and active. They lobbied hard at every stage: when this bill was studied by a House of Commons committee, when it was debated in the House, and when the Department of Justice drew up the regulations. We in MCCC wrote to the Members on the House of Commons Committee and again to the Minister herself. We recounted how a great deal of our organization's work in Canada and abroad was about helping victims of violence and war, and how our prison visitation programs and our victim-offender reconciliation programs worked with those who perpetrate violence. We called for a substantial strengthening of the controls.

Child Care

One time in the 1980s, the government set up a committee to study child care and to propose an appropriate policy. When I heard this, I contacted the clerk of this committee and asked whether we could appear. He happily agreed and proceeded to reserve a time slot for us. Then I called my colleagues in Winnipeg about preparing a submission. Some days later, they called back to say that it did not seem feasible. I then called the clerk to cancel our appointment.

He then expressed regret in a way that surprised me. According to my memory, he said: "I don't know much about Mennonites but my impression is that on the average Mennonite children are raised well, that your people have some practical wisdom about this matter that could help this committee to overcome the polarization around this issue and lead to good policy proposals and become beneficial to the larger society. I'm sorry that you will not appear before our committee and share your people's wisdom."

16

AMISH MILK CANS

♦

The Amish and Old Order Mennonites are well-known for seeking a more communal way of life separate from the larger society. Because of this stance, most of them have not accepted old age pensions, family allowances, employment insurance, or farm-related subsidies. For that same reason, they have kept their farms small, resisted mechanization, refused to connect up with the provincial electricity systems, and travelled by horse and buggy.

At times their way of life has not fit well with governmental regulations. On occasion I was asked to help them find accommodations. One such occasion involved the long-standing practice of farmers selling milk in eight gallon cans. By the 1970s, the Ontario Milk Marketing Board (OMMB) and its parent body, the Ontario Milk Commission (OMC), were encouraging farmers to install electrically cooled bulk tanks to replace those cans. This was happening in many parts of Canada. And many Ontario farmers had done so. It was said to be more efficient way of ensuring high quality milk. The higher cost also meant that it was better suited to larger scale farms than to smaller ones.

Then, in January 1976, the OMMB, which had a monopoly on marketing milk in Ontario, announced that after October 31, 1977 it would no longer accept milk in cans. Many smaller farmers objected to this change because of the cost. But the Amish and Old Orders

Amish Milk Cans

had additional reasons. They said: "We are all small producers by choice, milking our cows by hand. We feel this provides a healthy atmosphere for our families, a project for everyone, including ... the children." For them to become connected to provincial electricity lines so as to operate bulk tanks and other modern equipment was out of the question.

Upon receiving the announcement, the Amish and Old Order people talked among themselves and looked for alternatives that might be acceptable to the OMMB. In early September 1976 they made their appeal, explaining why they could not go along with the plan. As an alternative, they proposed the idea of a communal bulk tank. This meant that they would pour the milk from their cows into cans, cool the cans, and almost immediately take them to a centrally located bulk tank. There that tank would be cooled electrically but they, as individual farmers, would not have electricity. The OMMB would then buy the milk on a communal basis and they, as individual farmers, keeping records of how much milk each one had brought to the tank, would divide the money among themselves. They said such a system was being used in several Amish communities in the US and that the authorities there were satisfied. They also showed that even now the milk from their farms met the desired quality standards.

In the months that followed, there were developments in two directions. Inside the OMMB this proposal from the Amish prompted considerable discussion. An internal staff memo was quite positive toward the Amish proposal. Nevertheless, in a response of January 18, 1977, the OMMB rejected the proposal though its reasons were based on significant inaccuracies. The Amish then addressed those inaccuracies in a February 24 response, but the OMMB rejected this too. By this time the situation of the Amish was gaining considerable public sympathy. A Mennonite professor at the University of Toronto, Harvey Dyck, gained the signatures of prominent Ontarians including Pierre Berton, Rabbi Gunther Plaut, Marshall McLuhan, Judy LaMarsh, and Toronto Mayor David Crombie and presented them to the Minister of Agriculture,

William G. Newman. Also, many newspapers carried favourable articles. *Saturday Night* magazine observed that

> Tyranny appears in many disguises ... the OMMB is ... involved in a curious kind of oppression directed at the Old Order Amish dairy farmers in southwestern Ontario. The case threatens the religious freedom of the Amish, and at the same time casts a shadow over the pluralistic ideals of Canadian society. (December 1977)

By the spring of 1977 the Amish leaders were seeking help from the Kitchener MCC office, where Ray Schlegel was the Executive Director. I had quite a lot of interaction with Ray at this time about other matters, so he asked me if I had any ideas. This was soon after my lawyer friends, Ian Hunter and John Laskin, had helped to resolve the conscientious objector case of Thorbjorn and Bente Jensen. Would Hunter and Laskin be willing to look at this problem? I was happy to approach them. We then arranged a meeting in the Kitchener MCC office with about a dozen Amish leaders, enabling these lawyers to hear their concerns and the steps they had already taken in trying to resolve things.

As a first step the lawyers planned to appeal the OMMB rulings to the OMC. This hearing was held on October 18, but for unknown reasons the chair did not allow Laskin to cross examine the OMMB's key witness. If that had been allowed, then it would probably have become clear that the Amish could satisfy all concerns about milk quality and also that there were serious questions about the OMMB's stated reasons. Since that door was closed, were there other steps that could be taken? Hunter and Laskin felt there was an arguable case that the OMMB and the OMC had exceeded their legal authority and that those bodies could be challenged in court. The Amish, however, did not want that; they had always refused on religious grounds to resort to court action. What about the Ontario Ombudsman? Hunter, Laskin, and I then met with him, but he felt this was outside of his mandate.

As a final resort, Hunter and Laskin, on October 24, 1977 sent a long letter directly to the Premier, the Hon. Bill Davis. They argued that the Amish had no quarrel with the concern about milk quality standards; that they just wanted an opportunity to prove that they could meet those standards; and that if the authorities found that their milk did not meet them, then they would drop out. They also argued that the OMC was biased and that the issue was one of religious liberty. Their letter led to a personal meeting with the Premier and the Minister of Agriculture.

A few days later, the Minister of Agriculture met with Amish leaders and a compromise was reached: the Amish would accept bulk tanks but the OMMB would not insist that they be electrically operated; they could be driven by engines powered by gasoline or diesel fuel and they could be either on individual farms or at a central place in the community; further, there would be arrangements to avoid Sunday pickups and the Amish would be given a reasonable time to make the change-over.

When the Minister announced in the legislature on November 9 that a compromise agreement had been reached, he concluded his comments by acknowledging "... the valuable contributions made by the Amish to the social fabric of this province."

Obviously, my role in these developments was minor. But the story helps to show the broad range of governmental issues that arise from Mennonite life in Canada.

17

Organizational Maintenance Work

◆

No organization can devote all of its resources to the purposes for which it was set up; it has to devote some energies to maintaining itself. MCC is no exception. We in the Ottawa Office did not need to do a lot to help maintain MCC but we were involved in some efforts.

Tax Deductions for Donations
The right to issue tax deductible receipts to donors has long been vital for charitable organizations. It was important, therefore, that MCCC not get itself into a situation where it might be "de-registered" as a charity. One sensitive area related to "political activities." In early 1978 Revenue Canada issued a new "information bulletin" outlining the kinds of political activities that charitable organizations should avoid. A literal reading of this bulletin suggested that our office had crossed the line in a number of ways.

We then asked for a meeting with the key officials. We brought samples of our submissions on capital punishment, national defence, immigration, and other issues to illustrate our work. We wanted to be transparent. To our surprise, the officials were emphatic in saying that this was not what they had in mind at all, that they would not think of deregistering MCC. What we were doing,

Organizational Maintenance Work

they said, was more like expressing a concern or point of view, not exerting actual pressure, or "hammering" the government, or using threats, etc. The spoken words of the officials were reassuring, but the question of what political activities a charitable organization could engage in would come up again, even though the work of our office was never challenged.

A different challenge came up in 1982 from officials in the departments of Finance and Revenue. They issued a paper that suggested that the historic arrangement whereby people could deduct the amount they donated to church organizations from their taxable income should be reconsidered for the reason that it brought an unfairness to other Canadians who then had to pay more tax in order to fill the government's revenue needs. This suggestion raised widespread concern. Church administrators began to consult with one another about how to respond. I wrote a short paper for a meeting of church representatives with these government officials. In it I outlined in summary form the long and usually positive social contributions of churches, noting "day-care services for children, recreation programs, young people's activities, services to senior citizens, care for the handicapped and the weak, guidance for the delinquent, assistance to refugees, counselling for people in various situations of need, education programs of many kinds, alcohol rehabilitation programs, support for people newly released from prison, medical care for people in isolated communities, ... [and] a sense of belonging for many who would otherwise would suffer from ... alienation."

I then acknowledged that the government was giving a broad range of grants to various charitable organizations for work at home and abroad, often with positive results, but that the giving of grants was fundamentally different. To discontinue the historic system that helped church organizations to raise their own money by giving tax deductible receipts would, I argued, limit the churches' independence, restrict their creativity, and reduce the value of their contributions to society. Fortunately, the government dropped this idea.

Family Allowances for Canadians Serving Abroad

A long-standing part of MCC's approach has been to send workers to situations of need in various countries, in contrast to simply sending money to local groups. These MCC workers were not given a salary, but their housing and food costs were covered and they were given an allowance of maybe $25.00 per month. In 1977 it became apparent that some Canadian MCC workers serving abroad applied for, and received, the Family Allowance cheques issued by the Canadian government just as they would if they had remained in Canada. Other Canadian workers, however, were being refused. We were then asked to see if a consistent approach could be arranged.

We then inquired with the department of Health and Welfare, which administered the Family Allowance program. Officials there advised us that the key question was whether these workers were subject to Canadian income tax. To find that out, we had to go to Revenue Canada, where we learned that that question depended particularly on whether such workers could be deemed to remain "residents" of Canada for the purposes of the legislation even though they were serving abroad. This, in turn, depended on other factors including the control that the Canadian sending body, namely MCCC, retained over them when they worked in a foreign country. This latter aspect was complicated because, at that time, Canadian MCC workers assigned internationally were, in significant ways, under the control of the binational MCC in Akron, Pennsylvania, not MCCC in Winnipeg.

We then explained how MCCC and MCC operated and provided the officials with substantial documentation; we also appealed to a provision in the Income Tax Act that referred to missionaries. In 1981 we reached an agreement. It deemed the Canadians serving abroad under MCC to be "residents" of Canada for the purposes of this legislation and made them eligible for Family Allowances. But now they would also have to file income tax returns which, in turn, required MCCC to provide them with T-4 slips. This had implications for Unemployment Insurance and Canada Pension Plan deductions and led to further work. The original question was resolved, but in the process it had become more complicated for MCCC to send workers abroad. In 1992 the government replaced Family Allowances with other programs. Certainly, they were beneficial for the workers, but the organization, namely MCCC, now had to meet more complicated administrative requirements.

Provisions for Foreigners Serving in Canada under MCC
Though MCC sent workers abroad, it also brought people from other countries into Canada, under two programs. One was the Voluntary Service (VS) program. This program assigned workers to various social service agencies in poorer communities across Canada, usually for two-year terms. Most of the workers in this program were Canadians but some came from abroad, usually the US.

MCC had done this since the 1950s, but around 1980 officials began to ask if such workers were taking jobs that would otherwise be filled by Canadians. We argued that they were not, because of the very low remuneration, as described above. Officials conceded this point but they still wanted the workers to get work permits, or employment authorizations, as they were then called. We then arranged for MCCC to do this. As the sponsoring body it would apply for such authorizations for all of its foreign workers serving in Canada. The practice worked, for a while.

Sometime later, officials decided that the local organization to which the workers were most immediately accountable, be that in Newfoundland or in BC, had to get the work permits. This also meant that the government's decisions about whether to approve the applications for work permits would be made at the various regional Employment offices, not in a central office. This resulted in considerable inconsistency, which was problematic for MCCC; it could no longer be sure that if it found foreigners who were ready to go and well-suited for particular assignments, they would get the necessary authorization.

These and other problems kept us going back to the officials again and again. In general they tried to be helpful while still complying with their laws and policies. The decentralization on the government side contributed to a decision to decentralize things on the MCC side too, meaning that the administration for the VS program was transferred from MCCC to the provincial MCCs. Eventually, however, these administrative and other issues led many of the provincial MCCs to discontinue the VS program altogether.

The other program under which MCC brought foreigners into Canada was the International Visitors Exchange Program (IVEP). Approximately 30 young adults came to Canada each year under this program. MCC had run it since the early 1950s but by 1980 government officials were asking questions similar to those about the Voluntary Service program. Things came to a head in 1987. Fortunately, the government had provisions for exchange programs run by universities and other organizations. We then asked the officials to accept our IVEP program alongside those other exchange programs. We described the IVEP in detail and emphasized that MCC sent out many more people than it brought in. The officials responded positively and IVEP was able to continue.

Meat Canning Regulations
MCC has a long history of canning meat for shipment to areas of need overseas. It has a large semi-trailer truck with the necessary equipment which goes to Mennonite communities in both the US and Canada where meat from donated hogs and cattle is cooked and canned. In Canada these operations have been carried out in Manitoba and southern Ontario. They require extensive preparatory work and involve many volunteers from various churches and the wider community. Usually, the "canning days" have a festive atmosphere.

In 2005, however, just a few weeks before the canning was to begin in southern Ontario, the Canadian Food Inspection Agency (CFIA) announced prohibitions on mobile facilities even when they were temporarily attached to fixed facilities. The MCC canning truck was a mobile facility. The fixed facilities to which it had usually been attached included those of Winkler Meats in Winkler, Manitoba, the H. J. Heinz facility in Leamington, Ontario, and the University of Guelph in Guelph, Ontario. This CFIA announcement raised concern not only in MCC but also in the communities where the canning was to take place.

We then appealed to the responsible Minister to suspend the new regulations at least to allow time to seek a compromise. We also wrote to Members of Parliament. Many were quite ready to support our appeal because these events were popular in their communities. We also arranged a meeting with senior CFIA officials for which we brought in several MCC leaders and individuals directly involved in the canning operation. Before long, we had a compromise that allowed the canning to proceed.

18

MENNONITES FROM MEXICO

◆

*I*n the 1920s, nearly 6,000 conservative Mennonites from Manitoba and Saskatchewan moved to Mexico; another 1,700 moved to Paraguay. They wanted to avoid the assimilationist pressures of Canadian society, particularly the English language public schools that were being forced upon them at that time. However, life in these new countries was hard, very hard at times. As a result, there had long been a trickle of returnees. For several decades getting legal status back in Canada was easy; most families had at least one parent who was born in Canada before the exodus, meaning that they still had Canadian citizenship. And most of those who did not have citizenship could get "landed immigrant" status because the criteria for that were not very demanding.

By the 1970s, however, both of these factors were changing. Fewer of those who wanted to return had a family member who had been born in Canada, and the criteria for getting landed immigrant status (also known as Permanent Resident status) were becoming tighter in terms of education levels, language proficiency, certified job skills, and so on. Thus, soon after the MCC Ottawa Office opened in 1975, I received a request to help some returnees get status in Canada. This work became large and ongoing, with many twists and turns, but it was blessed with remarkable success, particularly in the area of "deriving" Canadian citizenship from the people's

Canadian parentage. (To have a "derivative claim" to citizenship is different from getting a "grant" of citizenship. People from the world at large have to meet certain qualifications for "landed immigrant" status, and then, after living in Canada for the required number of years and meeting additional criteria, they can apply for a "grant" of citizenship. In contrast, people born outside of Canada of Canadian parentage may, depending on certain circumstances, be able to "derive" citizenship from a parent.)

My own involvement in this work was intense at certain times but minor at other times. Workers in southern Ontario, Manitoba and Alberta—some of them under MCC and others working independently—did a lot of the front-line work, interacting substantially with local Citizenship and Immigration offices; likewise, workers in Mexico, Paraguay, Bolivia, and the US, related to Canadian Embassies and Consulates. For many years my assistants in Ottawa, who knew Low German, also did a lot of case work.

A Small Opening in Citizenship Law

How did it begin? In the fall of 1975, just a few months after the Ottawa Office opened, Rev. David Friesen from southern Ontario called to ask for help in getting secure status for a John Hildebrandt, who was born in Mexico in the 1950s. John did not meet the criteria for landed immigrant status and was in line to be deported, but the immigration officials in London, Ontario did not really want to deport him. They felt that citizenship officials should give him Canadian citizenship on the basis that his parents were born in Canada. David asked me to explore that option.

The Citizenship Act did not categorically rule out the possibility of giving citizenship to Hildebrandt. Passed in 1947, the Act provided that a person born outside of Canada on or after January 1, 1947 could be a Canadian citizen if (a) the person was born either (i) in wedlock and of a Canadian father or (ii) out of wedlock and of a Canadian mother, and (b) was registered before his or her second birthday. Unfortunately, John's parents, though born in Canada, had not registered him before his second birthday. However, the Act also allowed registrations to be done "within such extended period as the Minister may authorize in special cases." This last provision, giving the Minister discretionary power, allowed for what became known as "delayed registration" of Canadian citizenship.

After receiving David Friesen's request for John Hildebrandt, I called the Citizenship Registration Branch, which was then in the Secretary of State Department. The official I spoke to acknowledged that the law did allow for "delayed registration," but she firmly explained that their policy was to use that provision only for persons who demonstrated their intention to live in Canada by first becoming landed immigrants. I did not object to the requirement that people have an intent to live in Canada, but I argued that in Hildebrandt's case that intent was already clear and, further, that people with such close Canadian parentage should not be required to first become landed immigrants, because the criteria for that had been designed for a different purpose and had become much more demanding in recent years.

When I could not persuade that official, I asked, respectfully, whether she would object if I would submit my arguments in writing to her superiors. Of course she could not say no. I then submitted a letter on November 19, 1975 addressed to both the Minister and the Registrar of Citizenship. Two months later on January 20, 1976, the Minister, the Hon. Hugh Faulkner, responded saying that he had decided to make an exception and allow for "delayed registration" in the case of John Hildebrandt because he had certain health problems. But then the Minister restated the general policy of using "delayed registration" only for people who first became landed immigrants.

Obviously, the Minister held a narrow interpretation of the law but since he had now approved one case, David Friesen wanted me to try to squeeze in other cases too. He then sent me a shoe box full of papers, all in Spanish. At first I was overwhelmed, but then I bought a Spanish-English dictionary and began to study them. It did not take long to see that they were mainly birth certificates and marriage certificates with enough biographical information to enable me to sketch family trees. Some of these people, born in Mexico after January 1, 1947, were in the same legal category as John Hildebrandt, meaning that they might be eligible for "delayed registration," but others, born before 1947, were in a different legal category, one that technically had automatically made them Canadian citizens until age 24, as will be explained below. Unfortunately, they had not known about that nor had they known that they could have continued to hold that citizenship if they had taken certain steps to retain it before turning 24. Be that as it may, the legal remedy for their situation was to "resume" Canadian citizenship. Fortunately, under the 1947 Citizenship Act, "resumption" was also subject to the Minister's discretionary power.

Perhaps providentially, I had taken a university law course just a few years earlier that was devoted entirely to the concept of discretionary power. (The professor was Ian A. Hunter, mentioned in two preceding stories. He and I had then published an article in a law journal on the discretionary power of the Immigration Appeal Board.) This background gave me a certain confidence in now arguing that the government should use its discretionary power in both the "registration" and the "resumption" categories, to give citizenship to these people. In a letter of March 23, 1976, I argued that while it was reasonable to hold that such people should have an intention to live in Canada, it was not reasonable to hold that getting landed immigrant status was necessary to demonstrate that intention, given that the criteria for becoming a landed immigrant had been established for a different purpose and had subsequently become much more stringent. It should be possible for people to indicate that intention in a different way, I argued.

My submission, describing the families and outlining the arguments, accompanied by the many Spanish certificates of birth and marriage, ran for 17 pages. A few weeks after submitting it, we received a visit from Lorena Warnock, a citizenship official who would become an extremely valuable advocate on the inside. She had been given the task of sorting through our submission and preparing a response. Now she wanted to learn more about who we were and what we were about. She also wanted us to know that it would be some time before we'd receive a response. That it would take time was re-emphasized in an August 24, 1976 letter from the Registrar, stating:

> As a result of your letter of March 23, requesting special Ministerial consideration for a group of Mennonite families from Mexico, who are now back in Canada without status, we have undertaken an extensive research program. We have been contacted by the Department of Manpower and Immigration as well as External Affairs. Both of these offices seem to be giving serious consideration to the unique situation resulting from the exodus of Canadian Mennonites to Mexico. For this reason, I would ask you ... to bear with us a little longer in an attempt to find a truly satisfactory solution to this difficult situation.

By January 1977, the government had decided to approve our cases. But now things had to move quickly, because on February 15, 1977 a new citizenship law would come into force, one that would open some doors further while closing others. Thus, it was best to complete the processing of these applications now. With that in mind, Lorena Warnock and I drove down to Langton, Ontario where in a farm house on a cold Sunday afternoon all 76 individuals in our submission came before her, signed the necessary forms, and took the citizenship oath. We then hurried back to Ottawa, where she had the certificates made. She then gave them to me in a paper bag and I went back for another gathering in southern Ontario to hand them out. Now we met in the home of Aron and Margaret Wall near Elmira. Aron was an Old Colony *Vorsteher* with whom I had begun to work closely. They were renting a farm house where, on this day, the plumbing had frozen. But for these 76 people that did not matter; they were now getting the right to live in Canada permanently. After distributing the certificates and getting each one to sign that they had received it, we shared a few reflections and joined in singing the old Mennonite thanksgiving hymn, "Nun Danket Alle Gott."

A Wider Citizenship Opening, Albeit with Limitations

When the new Citizenship Act came into force on February 15, 1977, replacing the one of 1947, some doors allowing people to make derivative citizenship claims opened further. As noted, until now people born outside of Canada, after January 1, 1947, could be "registered" as citizens only if they were born either in wedlock and of a Canadian father or out of wedlock and of a Canadian mother. This meant among other things that the door was closed to people born in wedlock of a Canadian mother and a non-Canadian father. The 1977 Act opened this door. And it did so retroactively, meaning that such people, born after January 1, 1947, could now apply for citizenship, though there was a minor difference: instead of being "registered" as citizens they would be given a "grant," meaning that instead of being deemed to have been a citizen from their birth, they would be citizens from the day of the grant.

This new door in the 1977 Act was to be kept open for two years to give people born after January 1, 1947 a reasonable opportunity to use it. Since this was so closely related to the earlier "registration" provisions the government decided to similarly keep those provisions open for people born after January 1, 1947; in other words, to allow for their "delayed registration." These two provisions in the 1977 Act were referred to as "transition" provisions. During the two years that these doors were to be kept open for people born on or after January 1, 1947, the government would not insist that applicants become landed immigrants in order to indicate their intention to live in Canada. I had proposed that people be allowed to indicate that intention with a personal letter. Officials accepted that.

Though many people born abroad after January 1, 1947 could now apply for citizenship, there were limitations. One condition for eligibility was that they be born of a Canadian parent. The parent did not have to be born in Canada but had to have been a Canadian citizen on the day of the child's birth. However, as noted, in some situations this condition was intertwined with another condition, that of being born in wedlock. To illustrate, was it possible, if you were born in Mexico in 1954 to a parent born in Mexico in 1933, that you might have been born to a Canadian citizen and therefore be eligible for Canadian citizenship now after 1977?

In fact, yes, that was possible. The effect of the 1947 Act was that people born abroad before 1947 were automatically Canadian citizens until age 24 if, (i) they were born of a Canadian father, (ii) of a legal marriage, and (iii) were not yet 21 on January 1, 1947. Thus, people born in Mexico in 1933 who met these three conditions were Canadian citizens automatically until 1957, even if they had never applied for a certificate of citizenship. This meant that if such a person born in 1933 had a child in 1954, that child was born to a Canadian parent, making that child eligible for citizenship now, after 1977; further, according to the "registration" provision, that person—that is, the one born in 1954—was deemed to have been a citizen from birth, with the result that a child born to that person years later was deemed to have been born of a Canadian parent and therefore also eligible for Canadian citizenship.

What adds to the significance of this wider opening in citizenship law is that instead of closing it after the first two years, the government added another two years and another and another—all the way until 2004. This was profoundly significant. Tens of thousands of Mennonites benefitted from this opening. The government also dropped the requirement that people send a letter stating that they intended to live in Canada. We did not ask the government to drop this requirement but by doing so it was now possible for people of Canadian ancestry living in Latin America to get certificates of Canadian citizenship even if they did not intend to move to Canada.

The Born-in-Wedlock Limitation on Citizenship

Even though the door described above was quite wide, the born-in-wedlock requirement in Canada's early citizenship laws was a notable limitation. Until the mid-1930s, many of the Mennonites in Mexico had only church weddings which, unbeknownst to the people, had no legal standing. Mexican law, since the 1917 Revolution, had recognized only civil marriages. And international law held that the legality of a marriage was determined by the laws of the country in which it took place. As a result, a person born in Mexico in, say, 1933, of parents who were born in Canada but married only in a church ceremony in Mexico, say in 1931, would be deemed to have been born out-of-wedlock. Such a person would then not meet one of the three conditions mentioned above and thus not benefit from the provision in Canada's 1947 Citizenship Act of automatically being a Canadian citizen until age 24. This in turn now deprived that person's descendants from being able to make derivative claims to Canadian citizenship.

Interestingly, in the years following 1947 the Canadian government did not have a clear understanding of the born-in-wedlock requirement. As a result, it issued certificates to some people who were later discovered not to have met that requirement, meaning that they were not entitled to certificates of Canadian citizenship. In a remarkably candid letter of August 16, 1976, the Registrar of Canadian Citizenship acknowledged to me that "for some time the Canadian government was ignorant of the Mexican law regarding marriages ... and certificates of proof of citizenship were issued to persons ... who never had a valid claim...." Even after the Canadian government recognized that Mexican marriage law had to be followed, there was a question of what documents it would require as proof that people met this requirement. In a letter dated August 16, 1978, two years after the earlier one, the Registrar said that "statements given in an application concerning a parent's foreign marriage were normally accepted without question or attendant documentation...." In other words, if applicants stated on the application forms that they were born in wedlock, then officials accepted that. Even later, when the government began to ask for a civil marriage certificate, officials often accepted certificates made decades after the supposed civil marriage.

In later years Canadian officials became much stricter. Thus, when they'd receive an application, say in 1990, where the claim depended on whether an ancestor born in, say, 1933 was born in wedlock, they would often seek confirmation from Mexican registry officials that there had indeed been a prior civil marriage. If Mexican officials did not find that there had been such a marriage then Canadian officials would reject the application. This had implications not only for the applicant but also for the applicant's parents and grandparents who had received certificates of citizenship decades earlier under "more relaxed" procedures. Officials would now state that such certificates had been "issued in error" and were not valid. Understandably, when people received such letters they were shocked. If they were living in Canada when their situation was discovered, then officials were usually willing to draw on an unusual legal mechanism to resolve the problem in the people's favour but it took time and required additional procedures. Over the years I made a number of appeals for a different approach to the born-in-wedlock issue, but it stood and kept quite a number of people from getting Canadian citizenship.

Developments on the Ground

Despite the limitation that resulted from the born-in-wedlock requirement, the doors to making derivative citizenship claims that opened under the 1977 Act were remarkably wide. Lorena Warnock patiently explained to me how things would work and what application forms and supporting documents would be needed for each category, etc. I then shared the information with David Friesen and other documentation workers. In the spring of 1977, Lorena was directed to visit the Canadian Embassy in Mexico City. She also wanted to visit the Mennonite colonies, so she asked me to meet her in Cuauhtemoc and show her around. I had not been to Mexico as an adult but a friend in southern Ontario, Abe Wall, who had grown up there was willing to drive with me. The Mennonite people received us warmly. Henry Ens, a high school teacher from Canada serving there under the General Conference Mennonite Church, kindly showed us around. Upon my return to Ottawa, I worked in close consultation with Lorena and other officials to write a 15-page outline, "Obtaining Canadian Citizenship," as a guide for documentation workers. We then had it translated into German and sent it to workers in the colonies in different parts of Latin America, while citizenship officials sent the outline to key Embassies abroad.

Alongside the opening of these legal doors, there was a growing sense in MCC circles about the need for a service program in southern Ontario to help the newcomers with a range of issues. Already in the summer of 1976, Ray Schlegel, Executive Director of MCC Ontario, had asked me to do a brief study of how a service program might function. I proposed a program focussed on documentation, schooling, and health needs, to be guided by an inter-Mennonite advisory committee. The board of MCC Ontario approved the plan and our program started on March 15, 1977, with David Friesen and Eleanor Mathies, a retired missionary nurse, as staff people in Aylmer and Elfrieda Driedger as the staff person in Leamington. The advisory committee asked that I serve as chair. I had not expected that. But it worked, sometimes in English and sometimes in Low German. Since some of the people from the Old Colony church did not want their names listed as committee members we operated without a set membership.

As mentioned the Canadian government, whether Liberal or Conservative, kept these citizenship doors open until 2004. Why did the government do that? The law did not require it, and the idea of closing the doors was discussed among officials at various points since processing so many Mennonite applications was costing the government considerable staff time. Were the doors kept open because of the officials' personal compassion and humanity and the remarkable relations that our front-line workers had with them, be it in London, Windsor, Winnipeg, Ottawa, or at Embassies abroad?

Was it the appeals that we in the Ottawa Office made? Was it because of the considerable economic contribution of the returnees? In the later 1980s there were official reports that 85% of the vegetables in Ontario were being harvested by Mennonites from Mexico. We do not know what it was that led the government to keep those doors open for so long.

The fact that the government did keep them open led to an expansion in the MCC service program in southern Ontario and to the starting of others in Manitoba and Alberta. In Latin America, the work of independent documentation workers increased. My own involvement, however, decreased for some years, though I continued to chair the advisory committee in southern Ontario and to make appeals to the government on various issues.

It should be remembered that some Mennonites in Mexico, though eligible for Canadian citizenship, chose not to acquire that status because they felt that that would amount to abandoning the faith that God had called them to leave Canada and its ways.

A Small Opening in Immigration Law

As noted above, the Citizenship Act of February 15, 1977 opened very significant doors for us. But it also closed one. It tightened the "resumption" avenue. People who had once been Canadian citizens and who now wanted to "resume" that status had to become landed immigrants first. "Resumption" was no longer subject to the discretionary power of the Minister, as it had been under the 1947 Act.

This situation led David Friesen, late in 1978, to ask me to undertake another project. He had eleven families newly arrived from Mexico, where the parents had been born before 1947. Many had been born in wedlock of Canadian fathers, so they had been Canadian citizens automatically until age 24. This meant that for them the legal avenue was "resumption" of citizenship, not "registration." Unfortunately, the parents in these eleven families could not meet the criteria for becoming landed immigrants which was now a requirement for "resumption." As a result, they were in line to be deported.

My first response to David's call was one of hesitation. I recall saying to him that the government had already been remarkably generous to us and that I did not feel very good about asking for still more. David agreed that the government had been generous, but then he said something to the effect that "If you had sat with these people and listened to their stories the way I have, then you would know that you have to try." How could I refuse? He then sent me another box of papers with the details about these families, all in Spanish of course.

One reason for David's strong plea was that a different door through which he might have been able to help these people had recently closed. That door involved the Immigration Appeal Board (IAB). A new Immigration Act had come into force on April 1, 1978 and changed the role of the IAB, making it inaccessible to us. As noted above, in my university years I had done a study of the IAB, and David and I had discussed how to approach it. He had then taken several dozen families to the IAB in Toronto, always finding it sympathetic. Again and again the IAB had quashed their deportation orders and allowed them to stay. But that avenue was now closed for such cases.

Responding to David's new request, I prepared a substantial submission to the Minister of Employment and Immigration, the Hon. Bud Cullen. In a January 16, 1979 letter, I argued that the criteria and procedures for becoming a landed immigrant were developed for screening people from the world at large and that they should not be applied to these people, since they had very substantial connections with Canada, that the grandparents had all been born in Canada, that many of the parents had been Canadian citizens until age 24, and that the children born to them before they turned 24 were now in the process of getting Canadian citizenship, thanks to the openings described above. I also referred to various humanitarian factors and provided details about each family.

One result of making that appeal was an assurance that these people would not be deported while their cases were under consideration. But a resolution of their cases would take a while.

One reason was that at that time, in the spring of 1979, many Immigration officials were busy with bringing in the "boat people" from Southeast Asia. But since MCC was very involved with that, it represented an additional opportunity to build relationships with officials and to present another argument, namely that since Mennonite churches all across Canada were taking full responsibility for getting thousands of boat people from Asia resettled, why could they not also help these few Mennonites in a similar way? The government proved sympathetic to this argument. In a November 23, 1979 letter, Ron Atkey, who had become Minister of Immigration when the Progressive Conservative government of Joe Clark came to power in the spring of 1979, wrote:

> Although my officials have quite correctly pointed out that these persons are technically unable to meet, on their own, the financial requirements.... I am instructing that a broad view ... be taken and that the resources of the family, the community and the Mennonite Central Committee be taken into consideration in each case. In this respect your offer to have the Mennonite Central Committee provide to the Canada Immigration Centre ... a written guarantee of financial support for the family would be useful.

Despite this assuring letter from the Minister, it would take considerably more time for the procedural pieces to be pulled together. One reason was that there was another change in government: in the election in February 1980 Pierre Trudeau was returned to power. Another reason is that the deportation orders that had been issued to these people could not simply be disregarded. The law required that they be carried out, at least technically. As the months dragged on I pleaded with both sides: with the people to be patient and with the officials to move forward.

For the people this waiting was hard; they could not get work permits and health coverage, and in some areas, their children could not go to school. Some of the people then spoke to the media about their long wait. On April 29, 1980, the *Globe and Mail* carried a long story about them. This led one Member of Parliament, David Orlikow, a very well-intentioned man, to ask a question in the House of Commons. Later that afternoon I received a call from the Assistant Deputy Minister, Cal Best. Essentially, he said, "We are working hard to put together the pieces for a solution to your cases but legally it is very complicated, so it takes time. Also, what we are doing is so unusual that, if it is explained in the House of Commons there will be questions about whether these Mennonites are getting special treatment. We'd then have to drop the whole thing. So, please keep this matter away from the politicians." I then called Mr. Orlikow who, of course, was most willing to hold off.

Finally, in the fall of 1981, I was invited to a meeting where officials outlined the process to resolve these cases. (I asked David Friesen as well as George Rempel, who was replacing David in the MCC office in Aylmer, Ontario, to come up for this meeting.) The basics of the process were that Canadian Immigration officials would issue special letters to these people; with these letters US border officials would allow them to enter, for example, at Buffalo, New York; by physically leaving Canada their deportation orders would be carried out, technically; once in Buffalo the people would go to the Canadian Consulate and receive permits to re-enter Canada; once back in Canada, they would submit applications for landed immigrant status; these applications would then be processed speedily and on the basis of relaxed criteria, thanks in part to an MCC letter of guarantee.

Interestingly, the provisions for these relaxed criteria for "former Canadians" were placed in official Immigration Regulations; they remained there for the rest of the 1980s. One element in the willingness of Immigration officials to set up these unusual procedures was a commitment on the part of Citizenship authorities to change their law so as to again make "resumption" of citizenship subject to the discretionary power of the Minister, instead of requiring "former Canadians" to first become landed immigrants. Unfortunately, this change in the Citizenship Act was never made.

As for MCC's "letter of guarantee," we were also able to use that for the rest of that decade. It was for people who did not have a derivative claim to citizenship and who therefore had to become landed immigrants but were unable to meet the financial requirements for that. We in MCC would ask such individuals to seek the support of a local church. Since most newcomers were close to the Old Colony church, they would go there. That church would then agree to accept the actual responsibility so we, as an advisory committee, would recommend that MCC provide a letter of guarantee. As always Ray Schlegel, the Executive Director of MCC Ontario, and his board, were wonderfully supportive. During the decade that these special procedures were in place, perhaps a hundred families got Canadian status in this way.

Getting US Status for Mennonites at Seminole, Texas
There was a history of Mennonite individuals from Mexico going into the US to buy used farm machinery, taking it back and selling it in the colonies. A few had gone there to live and work for longer periods, with or without the legal immigration status. In 1977 approximately 600 of them purchased land near Seminole, Texas. They had received verbal assurances from American real estate agents that they would then receive permanent immigration status in the US. The majority of these would-be immigrants were from the Old Colony church near Cuauhtemoc, but some, including the leader, Rev. Henry Reimer, though also from Mexico, had been with the Old Colony church in Ontario for over a decade. A small number of these Mennonites were from other church groups in Mexico.

Another reason, aside from the need for land, why these Mennonites had gone into this venture was an anxiety about what might happen in Mexico. The debate during the 1976 Presidential election in Mexico had raised fears: might a new government take land from the Mennonites and give it to the campesinos; might Mexico, as the visiting American real estate agent suggested, turn communist? Not everyone believed this, but it helps to explain why some were persuaded to join the Seminole venture. This reason, however, does not explain why Old Colony people from Ontario bought into the scheme. For Ontario people, the attraction was to once again be farmers instead of wage earners and to live in a colony with their own people. With that in mind, the Old Colony people—those from Mexico and those from Canada—purchased a ranch of 6,400 acres near Seminole.

Not everyone was convinced that they would get US immigrant status merely by purchasing land in the US, but the first signs were positive. People from Mexico who started moving into the US early in 1977 received Visitor's Permits at the border, even when they came with trucks heavily loaded with personal possessions and farm equipment. The real estate agents expressed confidence that permanent immigration papers would be coming soon. Before long, however, border officials started turning people back, causing those already in the US to become anxious. They had made very substantial investments, but without immigration papers all might be lost. The real estate agents urged them to be trusting, but many became doubtful and began to seek advice elsewhere. One option they tried involved setting up a sizeable business called Seminole Mennonite Enterprises. They had been led to believe that maybe they could then become certified by the Labor Department and qualify for immigration papers on that basis. It did not work out.

During this time there was talk of a Private Bill in Washington that might simply grant Permanent Resident status to these people. Both George Mahon and Lloyd Bentsen, representing Texas in the House of Representatives and the Senate respectively, were indicating an openness to this. This was supported also by prominent individuals in Texas and by the sympathetic publicity that these Mennonites received. Even the prominent national magazines, *Time* and *Newsweek*, carried stories about them and portrayed them as honest and hard-working, if somewhat naïve, and suggested that for the sake of fairness they should be allowed to stay. Also, there were expectations for MCC, the most prominent North American Mennonite agency, to become involved. MCC was hesitant, in part because of the appearance of doing something for Germanic Mennonites that it could not do for Hispanics. At a certain point, however, Reg Toews, the MCC Associate Executive Secretary in Akron, Pennsylvania, felt that to do nothing was simply not acceptable.

Thus, early in 1979, MCC sent veteran Peter Dyck to make an exploratory visit. Then it asked me to do a more thorough study. Such a study, it was felt, could help get a Private Bill passed. Before heading out to Seminole, Reg and I went to Washington where we, together with Delton Franz of the MCC Washington Office, met with Senator Bentsen. He indicated that a thorough report would indeed be helpful for a Private Bill. I then spent a full month in the Seminole area. The situation was not entirely new to me. I knew a number of the people who had moved there from Ontario and I had stopped in Seminole on my 1977 trip to Mexico. But this project would be unusually challenging. I interviewed dozens and dozens of the Mennonites, as well as their lawyers, the real estate agents, and government officials, trying to get to the bottom of the conflicting stories. Then I went back to the MCC offices in Akron, Pennsylvania and wrote up a detailed 20,000 word report.

When it was finished in early June, Reg and I went back to Washington. We brought several copies of the report to the office of Senator Bentsen and several more to the office of Senator Ted Kennedy, who chaired the Senate Judicial Committee. That Committee had to approve the bill before it could proceed. Kennedy's office was most supportive. On August 2, 1979, the bill was approved by the US Senate. Getting it through the House of Representatives took more time, and more letters and phone calls, but it passed there on October 2, 1980, just before the Presidential election, the one which Jimmy Carter lost to Ronald Reagan. Some months later Jimmy Carter signed the bill in what was probably one of his last acts as President. The bill was a very simple statement instructing Immigration officials to grant Permanent Resident status to everyone on its list of 653 Mennonite names.

For me, this project was an intense experience. Many kinds of distrust had developed among the Mennonites; they felt betrayed by the real estate agents who had assured them that they would get immigration status if they bought land in the US; they also felt betrayed by their leaders for encouraging them to trust the real estate agents. And some felt ashamed of their own gullibility and poor judgement. For the Old Colony group there was another issue aside from getting immigration papers. It related to the 6,400-acre ranch they had purchased. Some months after making the deal, they found out that they had irrigation rights on only a third of it. This led some of the people who had committed themselves to buying parts of that land to stop making payments. Other people stopped paying when they were not allowed to cross the border into the US. A financial crisis resulted. They ended up losing much of the land in a foreclosure sale. For me to sit often late into the night and hear their heart-rending stories involving hopes, betrayal, anger, and remorse was an unforgettable experience.

Various church groups in the US and Canada took steps to be helpful, including the General Conference Mennonite Church in Newton, Kansas, the Evangelical Mennonite Mission Conference in Canada, some Old Colony individuals from near Winkler, Manitoba, as well as a group of former *Kleine Gemeinde* Mennonites from Arborg, Manitoba. Some of these groups continued to be involved there for decades. Likewise, MCC provided teachers in schools run by the Old Colony church there for many years.

The Seminole situation was unusual, but in subsequent years a number of Mennonites from Mexico have moved to the US; some live there without legal status. Their situation is similar to that of millions of native Mexicans for whom the prospect of a job and being able to provide for their families outweigh the risks.

The Citizenship Doors Narrow and Problems Emerge
In February 2004, Canadian Citizenship officials informed me that on August 14 of that year they would stop accepting applications for citizenship based on derivative claims from people born outside of Canada before February 15, 1977. Of course people born after that

date would still be able to make such applications but only if their parents, born earlier, had already done so. This was a substantial narrowing of the citizenship door!

Officials had planned to make such a closure already in 1999. At that time I made strong appeals against it. But now they told me that the decision was firm, that it had been approved by the minister, Judy Sgro, and would not be reconsidered. In fairness, this opening, which had initially been planned for two years, had been kept open for 27. After receiving this announcement, I took steps to get the message out to people in Latin America. As a result a good number—probably several thousand—who were born before February 15, 1977, sent in citizenship applications before the August 14, 2004 deadline, even though they may not have had immediate plans to move to Canada. By getting certificates, they enabled their children born after February 15, 1977 to apply later on.

Unrelated to the narrowing of that door but around the same time, two deep-rooted problems came into sharp focus. Both related to the loss/retention provision of the Citizenship Act that came into force on February 15, 1977. This provision stated that some people born abroad after that date who had received citizenship on a derivative basis would cease to be citizens when they turned 28 unless they went through a retention process. Counting from February 15, 1977, and adding 28, meant that February 15, 2005 was a critical date. After this date there would be people who'd cease to be citizens, thanks to the loss/retention requirement. The requirement itself was reasonable. Generally, it meant that people had to live in Canada for at least one year and then, while still in Canada, submit a retention application. The problems lay not in the requirement but in knowing about it and in knowing who was subject to it.

Though the retention requirement applied to individuals born abroad after February 15, 1977 of Canadian parents who were also born abroad, it did not apply to all such people. It depended on whether the parents had received their certificates of Canadian citizenship before or after February 15, 1977, and under which section of the law they had received them. But how were people now to know such details? Admittedly, when the government first issued certificates to people in this category, it usually sent accompanying "warning letters" stating that these individuals should take certain actions before turning 28. But the wording in these letters was not entirely clear and often the letters got lost in the intervening years. If the certificates of citizenship issued to such people had had an expiry notice on them, the way driver's licences do, then there would not have been any problems. But they did not. The certificates looked in every way as if they were permanently valid.

We had long been concerned about the loss/retention provision. In the 1980s and 1990s some officials then told us that they wanted Parliament to abolish it before anyone under it turned 28. Unfortunately, that did not get done, so as February 15, 2005 neared, we worked with officials to prepare publicity materials including announcements that we sent to workers in Latin America and placed in certain newspapers in communities in Canada. Our message to those in Canada was that they should check to see if their situation had certain characteristics and, if so, then to go to local Citizenship and Immigration Canada (CIC) offices to determine whether they were subject to this provision.

Incredibly, a good number of people who now went to the local CIC offices received false assurances. Many officials knew nothing about the loss/retention requirement. They would look at people's certificates and, since there was nothing on them to suggest that they were not permanently valid, they told the people that they did not need to do anything. Many officials used the phrase "once a citizen, always a citizen." The news of these false assurances circulated in the communities. Only later, after such people had turned 28 and sometimes only if they, for some reason, applied for new certificates, or for Canadian passports, did they learn that indeed they had ceased to be citizens when they turned 28. Understandably, they were shocked.

The people who learned that their citizenship had expired when they turned 28 represented the first problem. The second problem involved people who did send in retention applications before turning 28, as a number did, and who then learned that, thanks to the old born-in-wedlock requirement, they had never actually been citizens. In the intervening years, the government had adopted much stricter procedures regarding the born-in-wedlock requirement. To illustrate, if a person born in 1980, who had been issued a certificate of citizenship in 1985, sent in an application for retention in 2005, the officials would check to see if that person's 1985 certificate had been issued on the assumption that a key ancestor, perhaps a grandparent born in 1933, had been born in wedlock. If so, then Canadian officials would probably write to Mexican officials and ask them to confirm that, indeed, there had been a civil marriage between the ancestors in question. This took time—often over a year—and if Mexican officials reported that they could not find a record of such a civil marriage, Canadian officials would then inform the people that the certificates of citizenship issued to them years ago had been "issued in error." This meant that they had never actually been citizens even though they had had certificates of citizenship. This problem was not new but thanks to the retention requirement it now surfaced more often. And the legal mechanism that officials had once used to rectify such cases had recently been ruled out.

What to do with people in these two categories: those who now learned that unbeknownst to them their citizenship had expired when they turned 28; and those who were informed that due to the old born-in-wedlock requirement they were now deemed never to have been Canadian citizens, that their certificates had been "issued in error"? These were serious problems! If the letter of the law were followed, then people in these categories would have to apply for landed immigrant status. The criteria for this were very demanding and even if people met them, the process was such that for parts of it they might not have permission to work or be eligible for health benefits. And if they wanted to travel during this time they'd have to get Mexican passports etc. It seemed very unreasonable that people who had lived in Canada, often for ten or twenty years or more as citizens, working, paying taxes, running businesses, and so on, would now have to go through those arduous, costly and uncertain procedures as if they were applicants from the world-at-large who had no previous connection with Canada.

I pleaded strongly and repeatedly for a better approach than having such people apply for landed immigrant status. It took several years, and helped by some prodding from cabinet minister Vic Toews, officials agreed to deal with such cases in a better way: they would draw on a rarely used clause in the Act, namely section 5(4). This clause authorized the Governor in Council, meaning a committee of cabinet ministers, to grant citizenship to people in situations of "special and unusual hardship." (In a sense, this re-introduced an element of discretion into "resumption" cases.)

How would the 5(4) process work? What would be considered "special and unusual hardship"? In general, officials decided that if people had lived in Canada for a number of years on a good faith assumption that they were citizens, then the prospect of being sent back to their country of birth in Latin America would constitute "special and unusual hardship." The 5(4) approach was better than having to apply for landed immigrant status, but it was a great deal of work since officials wanted documentary proof of where the applicants had lived, gone to school, worked, who their siblings were, where they lived, etc., etc.

A Further Narrowing in Citizenship Law

While we were working on these problems, the government decided to further limit the scope whereby people born abroad could make "derivative claims" to Canadian citizenship. In reality, and despite the problems outlined above, Canada's laws for making derivative claims had long been generous, at least until the restrictions of 2004. Tens of thousands of Mennonites had been able to get Canadian citizenship. But some officials had long raised questions about this practice. Some said that those avenues extended citizenship rights to too many generations of born-abroad people. Others said that the inflow of a sizeable number of Mennonites was really an immigration and should therefore be regulated by the established immigration criteria, not through citizenship avenues.

In this context, in the spring of 2008 the government brought in a bill which, among other things, would establish the first-generation-born-abroad principle and abolish the loss/retention provision for people who were not yet 28 on the day it came into force. Such people would simply remain Canadian citizens. The abolition of that provision would be a major gain because it was creating huge problems for us. If it remained in the law, it would have negative effects for a sizeable portion of the people whom we had helped to acquire certificates of citizenship over the years. Admittedly, the first-generation-born-abroad principle was a negative aspect from our perspective. It meant that if you were born outside of Canada, after this law came into force, you would be able to "derive" Canadian citizenship only if you had a parent who was born in Canada. If you had a parent who had Canadian citizenship but was not born in Canada then, in all likelihood, you would have to become a landed immigrant before you could get a "grant" of citizenship, just like people who had no previous connection with Canada. This limitation of the derivative avenue for getting citizenship was significant, but the government's 2004 decision no longer to accept applications from people born before 1977 had already restricted the derivative avenue to a high degree. Most of the Mennonites in Latin America who could make a citizenship claim in what remained of the derivative avenue, and who wanted to do so, had already done so. And if they now had children for whom they wanted to acquire Canadian citizenship, they could do that by moving to Canada, even for a brief period and getting status for them here.

Passage of the bill was not at all certain. The government did not have a majority in Parliament. On the day that the Minister, Diane Finley, introduced the bill in the House of Commons, she called me. It is the only time that I ever received such a call from a minister. No doubt her advisors, knowing the bill's implications for Mennonites, had recommended that she do that. When the bill came before the House of Commons committee, the Opposition parties (the NDP, the Bloc Québecois, and the Liberals) seemed not to have a firm position. A strong word against the bill might have swayed them and led to its defeat, but if that had happened the government would probably have brought it back after the next election, which was called only a few months later. In light of these factors, and given the problems arising from the loss/retention provision, I felt it was best to support the bill and thereby have that provision abolished, at least for people who would turn 28 after the bill came into force. Such people would simply remain Canadian citizens, although they would not be able to pass any citizenship rights to children born outside of Canada in the future.

The bill came into force on April 17, 2009. This meant that we were still left with people who had turned 28 in the time from February 15, 2005 to April 17, 2009 and who, unbeknownst to them, had ceased to be citizens thanks to the loss/retention provision. At first I assumed that the government would want to resolve their cases on a "global" basis, but I learned that this would require Parliament to make another change in the Act. Getting something like this through Parliament would be difficult. I made a number of appeals for that, but it was not to be. This left the avenue of submitting applications for these people on an individual basis under section 5(4), meaning the "special and unusual hardship" provision which required so much leg work.

Another development around this time increased the need for this work. People travelling through the US would have to have passports. Until then, Canadian citizens had usually been able to travel through the US with just their citizenship certificates. Since border officials had no way of knowing whether a certificate of citizenship was valid or not, people could travel back and forth between Canada and Mexico even if, technically, their certificates had expired. Now, people would have to get passports before travelling, and Passport Canada had developed a method which, though quite imperfect, screened out many whose citizenship had expired. Thus, more people, when they applied for passports, discovered that legally they were not citizens. They now needed to apply to resume their citizenship. The "least bad" way of doing that was the 5(4) process.

A positive development in these years must be mentioned. On April 26, 2017 officials invited me in to say that they had decided to change their approach to the old born-in-wedlock issue. Specifically, if they now received an application for a new certificate from someone born in, say, 1985, and if that person's claim was based on a grandparent who'd been born in, say, 1933, but received a certificate in 1955, they would no longer automatically seek confirmation from Mexican authorities that that grandparent, born in 1933, had been born of a civil marriage. Instead, they would simply accept the decision made by the Canadian official in 1955 who'd issued a certificate to that grandparent in the first place. This change shielded a few people from having their certificates invalidated on the ground that they had been "issued in error," but its impact was minimal because of the restrictions imposed in 2004 and 2009.

Reflections on This Work.
Despite all the legal twists, turns, and disappointments described in this account, we were able to help a very large number of people, thanks to the provisions that were open to us in the years from 1977 until 2009 when the doors narrowed substantially. There would still be Mennonites from Mexico coming to Canada, but the numbers are much smaller. Fortunately, at present those who come can still receive assistance from what was the MCC office in Aylmer, Ontario but is now the locally owned Mennonite Community Services office, and from individuals such as Marvin Dueck in Leamington, who, after two decades with MCC, obtained certification as a registered immigration consultant. A few other registered consultants and lawyers also assist these Mennonites.

One common question is, How many Mennonites from Latin America received Canadian citizenship through these provisions in those years? No one knows exactly. Government officials have told me that they do not have numbers. Accordingly, in 2018 I wrote to as many of the Mennonites who had been involved in documentation work as I could contact in Latin American countries, the US, or Canada. Most of these workers could only provide estimates, but I analyzed their responses as carefully as possible and came to the conclusion that probably at least 85,000 people received Canadian citizenship certificates in the years from 1977 to 2009. (The way I came to this number is explained in my article in the 2018 issue of *Preservings* magazine.)

I believe that a substantial majority of the people who received Canadian citizenship have settled in Canada, particularly in Ontario, Manitoba, Alberta, and Saskatchewan. Certainly, they have faced adjustment challenges, particularly in relation to schools and various social expectations, but they have also contributed to the economy. Many, at least in their first years, did the hard field work of harvesting vegetables, but before long quite a few started businesses, some of which became large. At least one woman born in Mexico worked in the Prime Minister's office in Ottawa. Some who obtained certificates of Canadian citizenship continued to live in Latin America, but they could now get Canadian passports and travel more easily, for seasonal labour, family visits, business, or even MCC meetings.

In my 1977 trip to Mexico I met with Rev. Heinrich Dyck, the *Ältester* in the largest colony. I acknowledged that the church leaders there would prefer to have their people stay in Mexico. I said that we in MCC wanted to respect that, but we felt that some people were coming to Canada anyway and that therefore it seemed right that we try to help them so they could live in Canada legally. He said he understood, though he regretted the situation. But at that time I had no idea that the doors would stay open for so long. If Rev. Dyck had lived to see that tens of thousands were getting certificates of Canadian citizenship, what would he have thought? Was our stated desire to be respectful of their colony life in tension with helping people get Canadian citizenship? In the quarterly meetings of the advisory committee in southern Ontario we often talked about whether the availability of Canadian citizenship was "pulling" people to Canada or whether they were being "pushed" by poverty and other factors in Mexico. The individuals on the committee always felt that the "push" factors were much stronger. They would talk about the poverty that their families had experienced in Mexico, and expressed gratitude that MCC continued to help people get the necessary papers so that they could settle here. Some felt that by helping a good number of the poorer people to come here we were in fact easing things in the colonies in Mexico.

Regarding my own involvement in this work, certainly I made many appeals to officials, Ministers, and Parliamentary Committees, seeking changes in the laws, but I also worked hard to keep all interested workers informed about those laws. I sent out information, responded to questions, helped with all kinds of special needs and, for many years, hosted inter-continental telephone conferences where workers would share their experiences, learn from each other and identify issues, some of which I would then take to government officials. Keeping workers well informed was important because often there were false rumours about additional legal openings. Worse, at times there were unscrupulous individuals who talked about new legal openings, got people excited, and then, for substantial sums, filled in applications for hundreds of people and sent them in even though they could not possibly be approved. It was important that honest workers be as well informed as possible; it was also important that government officials know that there was a circle of workers who were entirely above board.

For most of these years there was a remarkable spirit between our workers and government officials. This was evident in London, Windsor, other parts of Canada, at Canadian Embassies in Latin America, and in Ottawa. Our workers would say that sometimes it felt as if the officials were our partners, just as committed to resolving human problems as we were. To illustrate, in 2015 I sent a note of thanks to a senior official in Ottawa who was retiring. I had never met him but I knew that my various 5(4) cases had crossed his desk on their way up to the Governor in Council. He responded saying: "Dear Bill, I take the liberty to call you Bill, as I feel you have been part of my life for the past 4 years and I write this in a positive way. You and I coming from different spaces and point of views have a similar goal: do the right thing...."

Conclusion

◆

Obviously, I have to be cautious about making evaluative comments, given that I was directly involved in this work, but I believe that many of these stories indicate that while we did not always get what we asked for, quite often our work did make a difference. In looking at factors that helped to bring this about, I would refer first to the Canadian context and the culture of governance. In my view it was such that many officials felt that, even though they were bound by their laws and policies, they had a certain "public service" duty to try to be responsive to groups like ours. This, I believe, is one reason why we had remarkable access. Admittedly, we did not always get to see the most senior representatives, but we were always given an opportunity to present our case. This had further implications. When one can sit across the table from a government representative, instead of being outside on the proverbial picket line, one will communicate differently. One will come with some understanding of the government's framework and of the considerations that officials and Members of Parliament have to weigh. More generally, in addition to the culture of governance, I would say that Canada, at least in those years, was relatively hospitable to Mennonite values. Canada was not a super power; it was modest in size and active in international development and peace-keeping; it promoted multilateralism and human rights. Domestically, Canada had a social safety net that, however imperfect, was helpful to many. In this context it was often possible to present our concerns, not as calls for drastic changes, but as requests for further steps in a given direction, for implementing commitments already made, for honouring the humanitarian elements in Canada's history, and so forth.

Also noteworthy is the support of the churches. The early fears that the Ottawa Office would cause division proved wrong. I did quite a lot of speaking and writing for the churches. And when I prepared a letter or brief for the government I would often tell myself that I should be able, if given an hour, to gain support for it in most of the churches. But it was not only a matter of the churches supporting our work. At times we could build on theirs. Mennonite theology has long supported the view of the church as a distinct body active in society. Thus, Mennonite churches, among other things, led the way in the private sponsorship of refugees; they pioneered better ways of dealing with offenders; they started what became the Canadian Foodgrains Bank; and, through MCC, they have had extensive international development programs. One consequence of these church activities was that the advocacy work we did in Ottawa was not based solely on ideas; quite a lot emanated from activities on the ground; and at times, instead of urging the government to undertake certain actions, I was seeking arrangements so that the churches could better fulfill their own role and calling.

Another reality, alongside such on-the-ground work of the churches, is that a number of individual Mennonites were serving in the government—some as civil servants, others as elected Members of Parliament. On occasion when I'd ask to meet with officials on an issue, I'd see a Mennonite friend among those on the other side of the table. I would then try hard to present our views in such a way that they would be able to use them in subsequent discussions with their colleagues. Often, when I'd write to a minister or senior official, if I knew of a Mennonite in that department, I'd send them a copy. On one occasion Jake Koop, a senior official in the Defence

Department, called me to say that he was just on his way to a NATO meeting and that he'd like to share a copy of a letter I had sent to his minister with his NATO counterparts. Needless to say, I felt honoured. Another time I asked Lorena Warnock, the citizenship official mentioned above, to check a draft of a letter I was preparing for her boss. To my surprise, her initial response was scathing. Only after several revisions did she offer what to me felt like a faint green light. But a few weeks later she told me that her boss had come to her saying, "We have another big letter from Bill Janzen; please advise me on how to respond." We ended up getting most of what we'd asked for. Another time, after an evening event downtown, I felt an inner nudge to check in on Bill Andres, MP from 1974 to 1979. When I came to his office, I found him in tears. He had just learned of a tragic death in his family. Years later I heard that he told others about how much that visit had meant to him.

Sometimes the Mennonite MPs would talk about the challenges of reconciling their faith with their responsibility to their constituents, and sometimes these discussions led to the question of whether Mennonite theology, with its strong emphasis on the church, has an ethic for politics and governing in the larger society. I struggled with this question and raised it with scholars. The historic Mennonite doctrine of non-resistance seems not to provide an adequate response. Nor does the glib dismissal of politics and governing as a mere "balancing of egoisms." In my view the work of helping to govern a society in ways that are reasonably peaceful and fair can be a way of following the teachings of Jesus about loving our neighbours.

But what are the principles that should guide the work of governing? Is it sacrificial love, as demonstrated by Jesus on the cross? Is it a sense of the common good, or what the majority may call for, or whatever may appear as just, fair and peaceful at a given time? None of these answers seems entirely adequate. A few Mennonite scholars have written on this question, but I feel this is an area where we could learn from other Christian traditions. If the

Conclusion

principles for governing were articulated more clearly, that would also, by implication, provide a clearer basis for critiquing the work of governing.

In the Introduction I noted that the Ottawa Office, and MCC's advocacy work generally, were started in a particular historical context. In some ways that context has changed. In my time, officials were very accessible and relationships with them were vital; now, they are harder to get to and more constrained by detailed policies. In my time, MCC and its ethos were reasonably well understood; now MCC is often seen as merely one of many "stakeholders." I was energized by the task of drafting letters and submissions that challenged the government and, at the same time, found substantial support within the churches. Now, quite a few churches seem more preoccupied with other matters. In my time there was a general hopefulness, both in churches and society, that despite some big problems, things were moving in a positive direction, and that supporting MCC and its advocacy work was a small way of helping that positive movement. Now, despite some good news stories, large and small, like some recounted in this volume, quite a few people seem overwhelmed, even afraid, and as a result many focus on their own immediate well-being.

◆

These and other changes suggest that the work we did, and the way we did it, belong to a particular era. But human selfishness and greed will continue to yield injustice and conflict in various forms at all levels. I would hope that when people gather and reflect on basic Christian teachings, they will still feel led to counter that selfishness and greed, and to work for the well-being of all—in whatever ways may be open to them.

About the Author

♦

William (Bill) Janzen grew up in a Mennonite community in Saskatchewan. He studied at Canadian Mennonite Bible College, a forerunner of Canadian Mennonite University, and at the University of Winnipeg. He obtained an M.A. from the Norman Patterson School of International Affairs at Carleton University, another M.A. in Religious Studies from the University of Ottawa, and a Ph.D. in Political Science from Carleton. From 1963 to 1966 he worked in the Democratic Republic of the Congo under Mennonite Central Committee and from 1971 to 1976 he was a part-time minister at the Ottawa Mennonite Church where he has been a member ever since. He served as director of the Ottawa Office of Mennonite Central Committee from 1975 to 2008, albeit with several 'leaves of absence' including two years in Egypt. Bill and Marlene have two adult children.

www.ingramcontent.com/pod-product-compliance
Lightning Source LLC
LaVergne TN
LVHW040058080526
838202LV00045B/3700